Lest We Forget

A

Collection of Verse

Published 2004 by Reva Publications
ISBN 0-9548164-0-4

Dedicated to my family and friends, from whom I have
received great encouragement.

Printed by
Infographics Limited
Tel: 01446 772428

Lest We Forget

A
Collection of Verse

He paws impatient at the ground, longing to get out

(see page 93)

Written and illustrated by

Thelma J. Lougher

Author's Message

I grew up in the countryside on a mixed farm of dairy, sheep, arable and market gardening. I worked with Shire horses and saw the introduction of mechanisation, respecting the motto "Good Farmers, Good Countrymen and Good Citizens". I have lived through times of changing scenes and values brought on by Government directives, with the influx of industry and urban culture to the countryside.

The loss of country people from the land, where mechanisation has replaced manpower, has contributed to the loss of country values, companionship and the core way of life. The remaining "stewards" of the countryside have maintained a healthy population of wildlife and habitats for the next generation, despite pressure groups and political threats.

I have put together a collection of country verse, which I have written over the years, giving an insight into thrills, thoughts, feelings and fantasies of country life that cannot be experienced in a folk museum.

I trust you will read and try to understand my reasons for writing these pieces. This is a book of thoughts and memories helping to replace the time or opportunity we often lack to reflect, enjoy and appreciate our countryside, together with its heritage and way of life.

A way of life not to be destroyed.

Part 1

Hunting Verse

*This section gives a wonderful insight into the countryside,
viewed from horseback and seeing wildlife in its natural surroundings.*

Part 2

General Country Verse

*This section is for the reader not interested in hunting but wishing to share
and appreciate the countryside.*

Part One

Hunting

And

Country Verse

In silence there astride my horse, I watched him travel on his course
(see page 63)

Summer Rest

Shading 'neath the branches,
Dreaming while they graze

Down in the meadow,
Where the stream runs by,
Accompanied by heron
And the dragonfly.
That's where the hunters
Wile away their time
Through those days of leisure
Wile the summer sun shines.
Shading 'neath the branches,
Dreaming while they graze,
Building up their stamina
For hunting days.

What A Day

More of a mist than rain I'd say,
And warm November air.
When raindrops shone like diamonds,
And jewels in the hair.
The valley still and silent,
The horses pranced and shied.
The day was made for hunting
And all were set to ride.

The pack had entered covert,
Soon music loud and shrill.
Rang out through the valley,
My heart with joy was filled.
No orchestra of highest fame,
Could ever quite compare.
With the music of the hounds
That floated on the air.

The atmosphere electric,
Ran through every equine bone,
Here the true born huntsman,
Like royals on a throne.
Though some were just a bit alarmed,
Their seat was none too firm.
This is when it sorted out,
The ones who'd much to learn.

For laying there before us, was
A hedge all neatly trimmed.
With parkland stretching out beyond,
And horses sound of wind.
A fox, all set to give a run,
A distant "gone away"
Oh what a promise this was
For, a memorable day.

This was how the day began,
This is how it went.
Foxes well in evidence,
With truly, scorching scent.
The season in its infancy,
The horses fresh and keen,
Days like this we think of,
When we sometimes sit and dream.

The Coming of Winter

When the berries of the hawthorn,
Hang in clusters on the bough.
The frost has touched the foliage
Gently, on the brow.
The garden's lost its glory,
The sunshine's lost its glow,
And all the winter sportsmen
Are rearing for to go.

The time when all the country folk
Are destined for a change.
Fishing makes a graceful bow
And shooting leaves the range.
The steeplechasing starts afresh,
The flat is in decline.
The evening calls for glowing hearths
A book and mulling wine.

The Upper Crust

Horses that are handled well, never lose their trust,
And in the world of horses, become the upper crust.

A horse is born a gentleman, a gentleman he'll be,
If born into the hands of those as gentleman as he.
Just so the filly foal will grow, to ladies nothing less,
If broken in by skilful hands and schooled then by the best.

So you'll find throughout the land, the horses much admired,
Are ones that fell to skilful hands, in spite of how they're sired.
Horses who are handled well, never lose their trust,
And in the world of horses, become the upper crust.

King of the Field

There goes a heart that is forward thrust,
A horse and rider bound by trust.
He's supple, calm, alert of brain,
Skilled in the seat with a light touched rein.
Over the furrows and over the rails,
Over the ditches he swiftly sails.
King of the field, on a horse that is game,
He swallows the turf like a wind whipped flame.

There go I when I was young,
Now I fear I am outdone.
Still I hold my head up high,
As I watch with envious eye.
My flame of glory, somewhat dim
In shadow of the rays from him.
To him, I touch my cap with pride,
He's more than proved that he can ride.

There goes a heart that is forward thrust
A horse and rider bound by trust

As time drifts by, this day'll be gone,
Here's a thought to cheer me on.
This lad will see, as I have seen,
Another youngster reign supreme.
He will learn with age and grace,
How to cope with second place.
So take your freedom, take the lead,
Enjoy your youth, your skill, your speed.

Never a thought has crossed his mind,
That these old fogies, lagged behind.
Were in their youth as good as men,
Who rode the country tougher then,
They have no wish, to take the shine,
From able youngsters so sublime.
King of the field, you take your place,
While we stand down with humble grace.

Excitement

What does the hunting horn stir in the horses?
Those with experience, who've hunted to hounds.
Grazing there peacefully out in the pasture,
Sudden excitement spins them around.

Sounds of the hunting horn, far in the distance,
Drift down the valley on crest of a breeze.
My! They're obsessed with it, galloping wildly,
Skid to a standstill, mane blowing free.

Look to their nostrils snorting and steaming,
Hot is the breath on the cold frosty air.
Off they go galloping, bucking and squealing
How they go wild with that musical air.

Look to the hoof scars that blemish the pastures,
Look to the foam that smothers the flank.
Oh, how they long to be there with the Master,
Hounds to the fore and a flight o'er the bank.

Who would deny them that wonderful pleasure?
Who can ignore the sound of the horn?
Nothing surpasses the thrill and the pleasure,
Riding to hounds on a fresh winter morn.

Monarch

Has anyone seen the mounted field?
Or sign of the huntsman yet?
All we have seen is the fox go by,
His sights they were forward set.

When the sound of a hound in the valley,
Echoed as clear as a bell.
Monarch gives tongue too freely for some,
He's a hound with stories to tell.

Oh, look to his skill when heading the pack,
He's bold and true to the line.
They flow o'er the wall like a waterfall,
They cover the scent like a chine.

Where is the huntsman? Where are the field?
Why do they tarry so long?
Monarch's away, the pack on his heels,
Hunting with wings and a song.

They're hunting alone, they're hunting bold,
That hound has never a doubt.
Holding the line, while gaining in time,
How he is mapping it out.

Who will be there as a witness?
Who will record it a kill?
Only old Monarch backed by his pack,
Monarch will capture the thrill.

Oh, slate him you may for his gossip,
Rate him they can for his noise.
Who would they have to show them the brush?
Oh, give him some credit now boys.

They flow o'er the wall like a waterfall,
They cover the scent like a chine

If you have never had the opportunity to hunt, I invite you to read the poem and imagine that it is you, sitting on the horse in the woodland. Experience the beauty of the countryside, the wonder of the wildlife in its natural environment and the invigorating experience of the chase, during the culling of the fox.

Snuffling their way through the undergrowth,
picking up the scent.

Relating A Day

Silently sitting astride my steed,
Relaxed, on a woodland ride.
Waiting patiently for hounds to find.
I listened, we listened my horse and I,
According to the silence
Even the trees listened.
My horse poised, ears pricked,
Everywhere was quiet.
Not a rustle of the leaves
Broke the stillness
On this still winter's day
Deep in the heart of the woodland
A rabbit hopped across the ride,
Unhurried about his daily duty.
Suddenly, the silence was broken,
By the cackle of a Jay
Laughing its way through the
Tree tops. A fox was afoot.
I knew it; my horse knew it,
A seasoned hunter, no fooling her!

Not a chink of the bit bar,
Not a flick of the tail.
Motionless, we watched and waited,
Eyes scanning the depths
Between the tree trunks,
Searching the undergrowth,
Scanning the covert.
Suddenly, I was aware of
A slight alertness of the horse's ears,
A minuscule movement of the head.
She had heard something,
Her senses finely tuned.
A slight rustle of the undergrowth,
Gentle cracking of the twigs,
Charlie was approaching.
He appeared, sneaking stealthily
Slinking swiftly through the covert.
His brush trailing like a rudder
Guiding him through the undergrowth.
The sight thrilled me.
Silently we watched this beautiful
Creature, a strong healthy fox
A picture to see. As he paused,
He cast us an inquisitive glance.
No need for a holloa! As we could now hear,
The music of the pack in the distance.
They were on, heading our way.
All of five minutes trailing their quarry.
The music of the pack rang out
Through the woodland,
We sat, taking in the pleasures of
The country life, the beauty of the
Woodland and the wildlife,
With the exhilaration, of the
Music of the hounds drawing closer.
The next thrill awaited us.
We had witnessed the way of the wanted,

Will the hounds run true to line?
Will the scent have drifted?
No wind to waft the scent off course.
A cracking of twigs, a rustle of undergrowth
Tells us the hounds are approaching.
The lead hound came into view,
Nose to the ground, dead on line.
Picking up the scent, snuffling their way
Through the undergrowth,
Little music now, with their concentration
Clued to the scent. What a sight!
As the hounds, one behind the other
Work out the line.
Just the odd puppy, raising its head
Following its leader, unconfident
In his ability to hunt solely by scent.
My horse containing herself no longer,
Excitement rippling through every muscle,
Prancing on the spot, champing
At the bit bar, nodding her head
Anticipating what was to come.
"Stand! Stand! hold hard"
Hounds now needing time and space
To map out their line.
Excitement or no excitement,
"Your turn will come old girl".
Then the sound of hooves in the distance,
The huntsman appears cantering down the ride.
Time to go, sitting in behind the leaders,
Skimming along the ride,
Bending through the tree trunks,
Brushing through the brambles,
Ducking beneath the branches.
She bends like a serpent, an old master!
This is where one has to be balanced,
Relaxed, go with the horse.

Full concentration on dropping
Alongside her neck, to avoid the branches.
At a time like this, one is glad of
The little horse, the experienced horse.
Swift and supple is the name of the game.
The speed at the rear of the field
Seems ever more increasing.
There's the odd occasion when,
All anchors drop, Whoa! Whoa!
A nervous shriek from the rear,
A horse, out of hand? A young horse,
Giving his rider a hard time?
These are trials of the game.
Out into the open country
Over plough ground, fallow,
Stubble and turf, heat rising from
The sweating neck and flank,
The neck strap working up a lather,
Froth exuding from slobbering lips,
Mud bespattered, lungs extended,
Cheeks flushed, adrenaline racing.
Here, we came to a standstill,
Engulfed in a cloud of steam
Rising off the horses.
The fox had won the day.
While, Charlie now steeped in the
Safety of his earth, feeling I am sure,
Much as we did, satisfied, exhilarated,
Puffed, another outstanding run.
A four mile point, an exciting day.
That fox is here to stay.
To hunt it's prey, to raise a litter,
Then likely to give us,
Yet, another good day.

The Fascination of a Fox

What is this fascination, we all have for a fox?
To see him in the morning, to sight him in the frost.
That golden brown in sunlight, touched with white and grey,
This shy and cunning animal, he makes a rider's day.

Country folk throughout the land, will always tell the tale,
How they sighted Charlie, while hunting in the vale.
Viewed him from the covert, wend his way through rush and sedge,
Pausing as he vanished, through the thickest briar hedge.

They always go too swiftly, to sight him, then to see
The healthy fox is far too sharp, for hounds, or you and me.
If only he would stay a while, when scent is slow and poor,
For every child that's in the field, to feast his eyes some more.

They never shall behold a sight to thrill them more than that,
Excitedly they tell of him, " much bigger than a cat!"
That fox, it was a beauty, to the child it was a dream,
The brush he had was simply huge! The best I'd ever seen.

Through his shyness Charlie's cherished, by hunting folk for sure,
By the careful culling they'll be with us evermore.
May the youngsters of the field, enjoy without the strife,
The pleasures of the countryside, preserving country life.

Snow

Silence falls on the outside world
When snow has settled deep.
No footsteps break the silence,
As the earth lies fast asleep.
A brightness looms within our walls,
The silver winks in fun.
It frolics with the brilliant light,
As the snow, reflects the sun.
It's good to know the log stores flush,
How welcome is the hearth.
Yet through us runs a shiver,
A tug at tender hearts.
Thinking of the new born lambs,
A birth, both tough and harsh,
That brings them to a frozen world,
Where snows conceal the grass.
We praise the shepherds of the flock,
No stauncher men, be fair.
They turn their backs on glowing hearths,
To tend their flocks with care.
They struggle through the snowdrifts,
Their muscles taught and flushed.
Give aid to those who fail with cold,
Bring life and hope and trust.
No hunting for the horses, who,
Stand fit there in their stalls.
These are deemed a blessing,
To aid the farmers call.
Brought out to the rescue, as,
They carry fodder through.

To places inaccessible,
To the likes of me and you.
With skill they take the shallow paths,
Their instincts mark the deep
Such power in their quarters,
Their fitness at a peak.
The hunting has its purpose,
To some it has its fun,
But to the hunting farmer,
There are duties to be done.

A Cross Country Ride

The feeling of achievement
And the sense of instant pride.
When riding through the finish,
Of a good cross-country ride.
The thrill of being airborne
The confidence, that's won.
Between a horse and rider,
Who are out there for the fun.
The horse is keen and eager,
The ears are forward pressed.
It's then you dream of hunting days,
Along there with the best.

Riding In the Vale

As we ride out through the vale to and from the meet,
O'er the common lands and lanes which make our journey neat.
We see what nature offers, as the seasons make their way,
And the constant struggle that we find goes on each day.
No matter what our views are, the facts they still remain.
Nature keeps her balance by the predators of fame.

The cubs are flushed from covert, before the seasons in,
Cornfields then are stubble clad, the harvest gathered in.
The wildlife taken cover from the corn fields to the hedge,
While all along the roadside there are seedpods on the sedge.
The hawk he hunts the hedgerow, he swoops from side to side
Always at the ready to pounce upon his prize.

Autumn still a youthful lass, the trees still full of leaf,
Cobwebs strewn they gleam with dew on moorlands and on heath,
As the sun emerges from the mists of early dawn,
The sun she climbs the heavens, her rays are bright and warm.
That's the time we make our way and leave the cubs to rest
Hacking home in lazy heat enjoying autumn's jest.

As the weeks pass by we see, the rapid changing scene,
Deciduous woods are changing to yellows, browns and greens.
The flocks are growing smaller as the lambs are all away
Ewes are turned to pastures new to flush for tupping days.
Ploughmen spread a fresh new look as autumn passes by,
Stubble melts beneath the shear, scanned by the seagull's eye.

Autumn winds now growing bold, while trees all clothed in rust,
Persuade the leaves to loose their hold, to join the roadside dust.
With every gust they scurry and scuttle for their life
Until they find a deep, damp ditch and quit the wayward strife.
Days in haste grow shorter now as winter comes in low
We all must take our chances with fog and frost and snow.

The elm trees in our valley for years have stood like kings,
Now we see their naked forms as life has taken wing.
Their ghostly outline sombre, majestic still in death,
Silhouetted by the sun while sinking in the west.
As weeks pass by we hear with joy a note that spring is here
The bleating of the new born lambs like music to the ear.

As the days now lengthen, no race to beat the light
The homeward journey gently paced, the schedule not so tight
Hacking home in peaceful mood the countryside serene.
Corn has turned the plough ground to carpets rich and green.
Birds they bustle through the day in haste to build their nests
Rooks will give the tall stark trees a dark and spotted crest.

The mating season now arrived, the hunting season closed
The foxes now are given a summer of repose.
Just as nature in her way lays down her code of life,
We must now respect the rules and cause them little strife.
The time has come for all to rest, Then oh, what joy to see,
The kicking of the horse's heels when turned to pastures free.

Lazing in the summer sun, by autumn they're refreshed, they
Long to hear the hunting horn their ears are forward pressed.
The fitness programme starts anew, so they can stand the pace.
They take their daily exercise the promise of the chase.
And so the seasons carry on. A cycle now complete
There's none compares to country life, or hacking to the meet.

*During the 1970s Dutch Elm disease swept through our countryside leaving a path of
devastation. One noticeable result was the absence of the cuckoo from the valley for a
few seasons.*

The Arrival of Autumn

When does summer really end and autumn then begin?
Some they have a special date and mark it with a pin.
Not for me, I cannot see a date upon the wall,
Depending on the weather, my instincts give a call.

Fruits they start to ripen, the big machines they groan,
As they trundle through the corn to gain their harvest home.
Everyone seems all intent while reaping of their toil
Fodder safely gathered in, while jams and chutneys boil.

The horses in the meadow still pestered by the fly
Looking to the stable yard, with longing in their eye.
Autumn faintly hovering, of grass they've had their fill,
There's no mistake about it, the nights are growing chill.

The puppies from the kennels are put out to their walk
This year's entries coupled and cubbing's all the talk.
The tack is all inspected, the stables spick and span,
Everyone is looking well from summer's healthy tan.

Then it all just falls in place, thanksgivings being sung,
It's then; I seem to realise that autumn has begun.
When it came seems rather vague, the year just carries on,
Each season has its magic, no fret that summer's gone.

We are upping our collars for comfort

The Bad Days

The squelch of the rain in the hunting boots,
Full to the very top.
We were upping our collars for comfort
With a warming, sip of Scotch.
The hollow hounds speak not a sound,
For not a scent be found
While the fox is steeped in comfort,
Well beneath the ground.

Slopping along through the water,
Squelching our way through the gates.
On to another covert,
Again to stand and wait.
Our flasks are sinking lower,
We're longing for a run
To warm the blood, despite the mud,
Before the day is done.

We pray for the sound of the hunting horn,
We long for the blow for home,
The weather is against us now,
No fox would dare to roam.
The light is fading fast I fear,
The day has seemed a week.
Oh, for a good hot broth and bath,
With a flickering hearth at our feet.

The vegetable dye in the master's coat,
Could not refrain from crying.
The coat it wept, so the colour crept,
Its quality was lying.
The breeches white, oh, what a sight,
They blushed a pucey pink.
The price he'd paid for tailoring,
It made him sit and think.

The huntsman's cheeks were flushed and red,
Lashed by the driving rain.
He tipped his brim, with a stiffened grin,
The day had been a strain.
Oh! This was a day to remember,
Not for the thrill of the sport,
For the day we got such a soaking
And the weight of our hunting coats.

Reynard's Ghost

A chill, chill night I have to tell,
When riding home from hunting,
A time, when I had given no thought
To the ride I was confronting.
With gentle stealth, a mist came down,
It swept across the moor,
Where bogs lay hungry in their wait
To capture fools on tour.

They are treacherous and fearful
To a stranger, roaming free.
But never caused the least concern,
To the locals such as me.
My eyes fixed firmly on the path,
There looming through the fog,
Every bush and clump of heather
Were my landmarks, through the bog.

Suddenly my horse, she froze,
Her feet set firm apart,
Nostrils snorting, fearful snorting,
I felt her pounding heart!
All my skin felt clothed in prickles,
Scalp felt chilled beneath my hat.
Frozen there, upon the saddle,
There we were and there I sat.

No threat could I account for there,
What terror loomed ahead?
That terrified my faithful friend
And tied my tongue, within my head.
Trying hard to give the leg aids,
Replacing now my silenced voice.
Reins and bit bar, useless metal,
Here we stood, with little choice.

Oh! What froze my horse in fear?
Laying eerie on an eve,
When we'd had, a good day's hunting.
Now my lungs could scarcely breathe.
Then appeared, this apparition
Floating on the still night air.
Gossamer so fine, transparent,
Is how I would this thing compare.

This ghostly form that hung before us,
Made its presence coldly felt.
"I am but the ghost of Reynard,
That you hunted to the pelt.
This is not a day of mourning,
More a day of thanks and praise.
When I took my rest eternal,
From the error of my ways."

Here, before my soul's departed,
I have come to bid farewell
And to warn you of the quagmire,
There's little room for you in hell".
Had my conscience doubted hunting,
Had I dreamt this fearful scene?
Sure, I must have simply drifted
In a distant, wakeful dream.

Though I'll never know the answer,
What a lovely thought, could be?
That Reynard, who was old and past it,
Came to send his thanks, Through me!

An Evening chase.

When the foxes hold their covert,
The hounds have failed to find,
The ones that slink to safety,
Leave no scent at all behind.
You think your day is ending
With no sport or true reward.
The Huntsman feels dejected,
With no task that he'll record.

The spirits then are lifted,
Chill of evening brings a change.
The hounds are heard to whimper,
As they fan out more and range.
Your interest starts to waken,
As the sterns they start to sway.
Someone gives a holloa
As a fox is viewed away.

It's then the heart is lifted,
As it quickens up its pace.
A look of instant pleasure,
Seems to creep across one's face.
The girth is re-adjusted,
Your cap is set on firm.
You bring your horse together,
As you make a for'ard turn.

Should the fox be heading,
A direction far from home.
Should you see the sun is set,
Upon a sinking throne.
Would you be a sportsman,
To surrender to the time.
And set off to your stable yard,
Your spirits in decline.

I am sure, the truest sportsman,
Is the one who joins the run,
Not a second thought would he
To any sinking sun.
When the chase is over,
The huntsman bids good night,
Full well you know your landmarks
Are furthest from your sight.

You make your way cross-country,
You'll make it right and straight.
Trying not to linger, or
Tarry at the gates.
When you start to recognise,
The silhouettes and walls.
Then the pace is slackened off,
The chase is then recalled.

This is sheer fulfilment, of
A thrilling, evening chase.
An extra added bonus that
Dims the hours of waste.
For those who quit the hunting field,
The hour the sun was set.
Had not enjoyed fulfilment,
They only felt, regret.

The ones who'd had the greatest time,
Were those who rode it all.
Hacking home at twilight,
They saw the curtains fall.
Their final journey mantled,
By a canopy of stars.
Never do I envy those,
With boxes on their cars.

A Hunting Alphabet

A   is for arrogance, from which you refrain,
essential out hunting to get a good name.

B   is for bumptious, a trait they dislike,
more to the point it is get on your bike.

C   is for check, when hounds lose the line,
C is for Chase when conditions are fine.

D   is for damage; you must not ignore,
that's if you wish to go hunting once more.

E   is for etiquette; one must respect,
while riding to hounds in the dry or the wet.

F   is for field and friendship and fox,
footies and followers, fences and flocks.

G   is for gates we aim to keep shut,
When trailing behind, then close them you must.

H   is for hunting, while culling the fox,
A part of our heritage not to be lost.

I   is for instinct, the key to the game,
while riding to hounds like an oil fired flame.

J   is for jumps that stand in your way,
failing to ride them ruins the day.

K   is for keepsake, received with much pride,
when first at the kill from a long, hard ride.

L   is the line, on which you will hunt,
far more exciting when ridden up front.

M   is for Master, who takes all the brunt,
noted to frown upon any wild stunt.

N is for nerve and plenty you'll need,
to ride across country at true hunting speed.

O is the Opening Meet of the year,
one at which most of the followers appear.

P is for pride you take in your dress;
the horse and your turn out you give of your best.

Q is for quagmire that lays there concealed,
intent there to capture a few of the field.

R is the rascal, who gallops in fun,
without a straight goer, should never be done.

S is for silence, one tries hard to keep,
to listen to hounds, when starting to speak.

T for the thruster, who fails to hold back,
steeped in his ignorance crowds on the pack.

U for unsightly, when dressed incorrect,
a tie blowing free will spoil the effect.

V for the vixen with shrill sounding scream,
that raises her cubs in the gorse-land scene.

W for the whip, who brings the hounds back,
if any should venture and stray from the pack.

X is for Xmas, Christmas in short,
that is the time when we all love our sport.

Y is for yellow, the colour of some,
when faced with an obstacle, during a run.

Z is for zest, with which you should hunt,
when riding to hounds to stay with the front.

Competitors

We must have good competitors who aim there for the prize.

What is this urge that some men have,
To win at any cost?
That kills the fun for everyone,
Near them, when they've lost.

We all must try our very best,
It's good to aim up high.
But if you lose, then give a smile,
And have another try.

Many people try so hard!
To win a first rosette.
Yet how much fun there can be
Won, just giving of your best.

For everyone who gets a prize,
There could be twenty more,
Who set their mind on winning,
And feel a little sore.

What a lot of misery,
Just one event could bring.
If all were poor sportsmen,
And only out to win.

Our Hunting Scene

We see amongst us racing men,
With point-to-pointers sleek

Our hunting field made up of folk,
Their set you clearly see.
The hunting staff with ribboned caps,
And hounds there close at heel.
Then we have the earnest band,
The farmers want their prey.
The lambing season's drawing near,
They cannot lose a day.
The rouge fox, yes, he must be found,
Culling must be done.
Or sure enough the fox's fate
Will be the snare and gun.
Neither these are God's own way,
The hunting must prevail.
To keep the foxes healthy
And thriving in the vale.

We see amongst us, racing men,
With point-to-pointers sleek,
As one by one they qualify,
They drop out week by week.
Professional men.
You'll pick them out,
They choose the better days,
To seek escape from stress and strain
To breathe the country ways.
You'll find, we have those country girls,
To businessmen are wed.
Spend some time among her roots,
At three o'clock she's fled!
Returning home to take her place,
Besides the kitchen sink,
To tend the children, cook the meals,
Refreshed her cheeks all pink.
Then we have the horsey set,
Who spend their working days,
Schooling, teaching, breaking-in,
That's how they earn their pay.
Our local Vets, we have a few,
They choose to take their rest,
They share the thrill of hunting,
Along there with the best.
The Christmas break, the children come,
They swell the mighty flood,
Excitement carries them all day,
All woolly, sweat and blood.
Never a thought to their scratches,
Gathered on their way.
Those are purely hallmarks,
Of a true fantastic day.

Memories

There were good days and bad days,
Slow days and fast days.
Days to remember and days that were scotched.
Days that I wished would go on forever,
Days when I wistfully looked to my watch.

Days that have stayed with me,
Deep in my memory,
Giving me pleasure, pleasure untold.
Stories to tell of, I love to remember,
Tell to the grandchildren, now I am old.

Days when I rode on that mare that I treasured,
Crossing the countryside, fleet as the wind.
Holding position, in view of the hunting.
Taking in stride all the hedges and rails.

Oh, how I loved it, the thrill of the hunting field,
Oh how I still hear the cry of the hounds.
Music, such music! I'll always remember,
Ring in my ears, now deaf to the sounds.

Oh how I loved it, the skill of the huntsman,
How I remember the wind and the rain,
Never as chill winds, just tingling memories,
Speeding my blood as it seeps through my veins.

Now that I'm sitting here close to my fireside,
Stiff in the limbs that ended my sport.
Still I go hunting, the good days, not bad days.
Tell of my memories until I am hoarse.

The gunmen standing at their post,
Their eyes were fixed the dogs lay close.

The Predators of Country Fame

I remember the cornfields, gold and clean,
With a piece stripped bare near the woodland green,
Where rabbits ventured out at night
Who dined in state, in the pale moonlight.

All good things come to an end,
The binder was, I fear no friend,
To animals who lived and dined,
Within the cornfields on my mind.

The day would come to reap and mow,
The company would grow and grow,
Invited sportsmen, cap and gun,
All intent, if game should run.

On the corners at their post,
Their eyes were fixed their dogs lay close.
Their prey was rabbit, fox and game,
All predators of country fame.

Our Faithful Friends

Dressage or eventers, or a horse to pull a cart

Horses they can vary, in colour shape and shade,
Anything from chestnut through to appaloosa, greys,
Dark bay, light bay, mid bay, bright bay,
Varying degrees there are, of liver, brown and black,
Then there is the type of horse, hunter, cob or hack.
Well bred thoroughbreds, point to pointers sharp,
Dressage, and eventers, or a horse to pull a cart.
Some are bred for temperament, some are bred for bone,
Others never bred at all, the mares just simply roamed.
Pony types are many, from the hills and from the vales.
The mountains and the moorlands the forests and the dales
Their faithful friends to children, who bubble forth with tales
Of those little characters who venture forth from Wales.
There are piebalds, skewbalds, palomino, duns.

Little riders need some pluck, to hold them on a run.
Horses come in large or small, some are dressed complete,
Shaggy in their winter coats, others clipped and neat.
There's the full clip, trace clip, blanket clip and trim,
Horses fed on grass and hay, others oats fed to the brim.
Well groomed thick manes, flowing in the wind.
Hogged manes, pulled manes, plaited, stitched and trimmed.
There is a sprinter, a stayer, a plodder and a swayer,
Some with their ears pricked the best view in the land.
All in all, we have to say, what matters really on the day,
The smartly turned out look the best,
But can your horse stay with rest?
If he keeps you in the front,
What matters if your nag's a runt
We love, yes love our faithful friend,
And nothing will our friendship end.

This is Dobbin

Time to Go.

When the stubble spreads before us,
Like a pinstriped yellow plain.
The barns are to the rafters,
With the flint like golden grain.
The cattle look to lattermath,
With longing in their eyes,
The summer pastures rather sparse,
The swallows set to fly.
That's the time to up and go,
A longing in our veins,
We check out all the hunting tack
And supple up the reins.
The cubs are full of vigour,
The ewes are put to tup.
Now's the time to tally ho!
And stir the litters up.

Dreaming of the future

The Whip

Sited to advantage,
to where the fox might break

The whip rides 'round the covert from the huntsman at the draw
Alert and keen he views the scene, clutching every straw.
Silently astride his horse peering through the gate,
Sighted to advantage to where the fox might break.
With a piercing tally ho! He signals Charlie's flight
Planning now the swiftest line to keep him in his sight.
The huntsman having made his ground and ridden to the frame,
The whip turns his direction and heads off down the lane.
His sights are set cross-country, he's swift along the route,
Aiming to regain a view of hounds well in pursuit.
A good man knows his fox, he thinks fox what is more,
As long as they don't head him he'll view them on the moor.
Another of his arduous tasks, is to bring the pack together,
Should they set upon a brace in fast and screaming weather.
Whipping up the stragglers, taking all the flack,
If the huntsman's beaten by a headstrong splitting pack.
Their job is hard and vigorous with little thanks and praise
Up at crack of dawn are they with small and meagre pay.
Dedication is the game, ambition being the driver,
This one takes it in his stride he never was a skiver.
His dream to be a huntsman, some make it others nay,
Many have this cherished dream but fall along the way.
If by chance he makes it, then another dream will dawn,
Huntsman of a famous pack to carry a famous horn.

This is a pony whose mother got a little excited when her foal was born
She nibbled off the top of his ear. What a character!

Here's to the pony who gives them a day,
And stays in the hunt the whole of the way

To the Ponies

Here's to the ponies who gallop to hounds,
Their little legs strive to cover the ground.
Their spirit is bold my word they are tough,
Their bellies they heave as they stop for a puff.

Oh how they show the big ones the way,
When taking a jump, so rare will they sway.
They gallop along a mere belly high,
The arrogant large look down on the shy.

So, here's to the pony that gives them a day,
And keeps in the hunt the whole of the way.
While giving his rider the thrills of the chase.
Splattered with mud with a beaming, red face.

Here's to the pony, who's hardy and bold,
Covered in feather, a handful to hold.
That is the one to teach them to ride.
Those with no talent they'll put by the side.

Hunting Dress

Hunting Red with silk top hat,
White stock with plain gold pin.
Breeches white but not too tight,
With everything tucked in!
This is dress for hunting staff
And members of the club,
Black leather boots with brown trim tops,
And nicely laundered gloves.
Now the times are changing,
When safety's all the thing.
What good is hunting silk they say
While dangling on a string?
Now crash caps are an option,
They protect you in a fall
But you must dress them smartly
In a black or navy caul.
Coats and caps in matching black.
That's farmer's own attire,
But ribbons dangling down the back,
Will cause a line of fire.
Should you wear a hunting cap,
Ribbons you conceal,
For they depict the hunting staff,
And masters on the field.
For followers the coats are black
Or could be navy blue,
Worn with britches fawn or buff,
The gloves a beigey hue.
With that you wear a bowler
Well, if you've come of age
Ladies and the gentlemen,
Of that mature stage

Children they are quite correct,
In fawn and bluey tweeds.
With jodhpur boots all polished neat,
And gaiters to the knees.
One never really likes to see,
The horse dressed like a Christmas tree.
With gaudy colours on the tack
It's best to stick to brown or black.
Of course there is the sheepskin too
But best avoid the reds and blues.
For the ladies, best be plain,
Mascara dribbles in the rain!

Summer Pastimes

Summer is the season,
When hunting takes a rest.
We turn to other pastimes,
To which we give our best.
There is gardening and cricket,
The racquet and the ball,
You can bet, whatever,
It's a pastime that will call,
For energy and effort,
And a lively way of life,
Building jumps or organising,
Gymkhanas and the like,
There are very few true hunting folk,
Who waste their hours of fun.
They're mostly, such enthusiasts,
They're always on the run.

A hose pipe is a blessing, in these trying evening hours

*(Frowned upon by the old grooms, who were
lucky enough to work on the lighter ground!)*

An Ode to the Hose Pipe

When the fox has steered the hunting,
Through the quagmire and the clay.
Has given the horse and riders,
A hard and tiring day.
You can ford the river crossing,
You can splash about up stream,
Yet still the horses bellies,
Caked in clay like slimy cream.
There's a kicking and a lashing
If this fiend be left to dry.
Harsh would be the treatment,
While the grooms have cause to cry,

Returning to the homestead,
It's a currycomb and shower,
A hose pipe is a blessing
In these trying evening hours.
A rub down with a scraper,
A thatch of good old hay,
A good bran mash be fair reward,
To finish off the day.
Those who hunt the gravel,
Or the sand or marl or loam,
Will never know the hardship,
Of a hunter going home.
When they've hunted in the valleys
On the blue and yellow clay,
The lime soil has a biting sting,
And mud rash rules the day.
So we bless the handy hose pipe
Pile deep the straw and hay.
With happy horse, the riders then,
Can reminisce the day.

The Castle Siege

The river ran its sleepy path,
Beneath the wooded, slope.
While high upon the hilltop.
The mighty castle groped.
Smothered there midst scrub and trees,
All taken hold in time.
They served to be protection,
For this castle in decline.

The fortress with its sturdy walls,
Now crumbling with decay.
The battlements in part disguise,
Concealed there by the way.
With ivy, hung in deep cascades,
Like robes of richest green.
Which proved a host for wild life,
A safe protective screen.

No knights in armour marched around,
No drawbridge chains to groan.
No merriment from mead to hail
Supporters, of the throne.
The swords have long since lain to rest,
The molten lead gone cold.
Peaceful now the castle lies,
Compared with days of old.

But this day, things were different,
Reynard chose to run, he,
Set the pace a grand old race,
And gave us all our fun.
He took us through the pastures,

Then slinking through the copse
Swam across the river while
He skirted town and shops.

Dodged the traffic by the zoo,
And thought how glad was he.
Unlike the animals inside,
That he was fit and free.
He took us down the valley,
Crossed the river in his flight,
Led the hounds to the castle grounds,
Then vanished out of sight.

The fortress had its own defence,
There amidst its towers,
Flocks of birds as look out,
Peeping from the bowers.
They sang and chirruped so to say
"Intruders making ground"
While Charlie sat in safe retreat,
High above the ground.

There outside these ancient walls,
Was set this brilliant scene.
Hounds tried hard to scale the heights
They stretched aloft and screamed.
The huntsman in his scarlet coat,
Upon the horn did blow,
Advancing, as the soldiers did,
With bugles long ago.

The whip, called off the eager hounds,
Who scaled the crumbling walls.
While all the field who backed the siege,
Had feared that they should fall.

The horses like the cavalry,
No armour clad had they.
They played their part as actors in,
This pageant of the day.

The front line were the footies,
Surrounding all the walls.
The fox, he was the knight of old,
Who heard the bugle calls.
The stage now set, the siege was nigh
The hunted out of sight.
Not a hope had they to catch,
This cunning, mocking knight.

This scene was like a pageant,
As actors would enact,
Though all had been impromptu,
Involving all the pack.
One actor gained a top award,
Prime victor of the day.
The fox, our knight, no armour clad,
Who set up this display.

The only tragedy to tell,
No film crew were to hand,
Recording there the pageant that,
The fox had solely planned.
But all of us remember
But should our memory fail
These pages bring back memories
Along with, a glass of ale.

Manners

Manners, oh manners, the making of man,
Take them out hunting, whenever you can.
Touching your cap to the man on the gate,
Standing one side for the huntsman and wait.
Encouraging youngsters, help when you can.
Never annoy a hard working man.
Always send word if cars wish to pass,
Do of your best to get on the grass.
But if you see grass that is carefully mown,
To scar it with hoof marks, will cause folk to groan.

Then there's the farmer, a fine patient man,
Show him respect whenever you can.
By closing his gates, consider his stock,
Never, oh never just tear through his flock.
Treat every field that you come to with care,
Seed and new leys are the ones to beware.
Galloping only in heat of a chase.
Hunting should never be cause for a race.
Giving fair play to a horse at a fence,
Thrusting's despised of, please use your good sense.

Skill is the key to the speed that you gain,
Safe at the kill is the prize that we aim.
Manners out hunting are always a must,
Never leave room for an ignorant crust.
Bid your good morning and bid your good night,
It's never a crime to show you're polite.
Hunting has come to us down from the past,
We are custodians, long may it last.
We hunt at the goodwill of country folk,
I pray you good people they're never provoked.

Food for Thought

He'll feed himself I have no doubt,
From off the forest floor.

While riding out one evening
Midst autumn's brilliant blaze,
I chanced upon a vision,
A fox beheld my gaze.
Mooching there beneath an oak,
His coat and leaf in tone.
I revelled at the spectacle,
From on my equine throne.

An autumn rust, in evening sun,
His coat beheld my gaze.
Toning in with early fall,
He paused, with one foot raised.
Aware now of my presence,
He did not seem on edge.
He first returned my saucy stare,
Then, slipped off through the hedge.

This picture left me, deep in thought
While riding on my way.
I'll know that fox, I am quite sure,
We'll meet another day.
Then I fear, on different terms
When all will be intent,
When he will set a lively pace,
While hounds map out his scent.

As a rider of the field,
When tightening up my girth,
I'll wish him secretly, God speed,
Safely, to his earth.
He's not the one to bother us
Around the hen house door,
He'll feed himself I have no doubt,
From off the forest floor.

The old fox that is past his prime,
Comes searching for his prey.
With his skill he'll give a chase,
But lack the power to stay.
That's the Reynard we will hunt,
Intent to put to rest.
Before he strips our chickens,
Of the liver from their breasts.

Hound Puppies

The saucy one is more than pleased
to poke about and strut

There is a litter at the kennels,
They'll soon be placed to walk.
One dear chap is quite content,
To sit around and talk.
The one whose tummy's rather full,
Just sits upon his butt!
The saucy one is more than pleased,
To poke about and strut.
Some just snuggle in their beds,
A most contented sight,
Gentle little darlings,
Not ones to pick a fight.
The conceited Mr. Handsome!
He has the tri-tone touch,
With conformation, charm and looks,
With an attitude as much.

Every one a darling,
But what is most defined,
Each one I can assure you,
Has an independent mind!
You can take them as a couple,
They will wile away the hours.
Though, I wouldn't like to speculate
The state, of lawns and flowers.
Take an individual,
Mark my words, yes, he will be,
A very faithful caller,
At the door for Hunting Tea!

This dear chap is quite content to sit around and talk.

The Beauty of Youth

One thing that will cross your mind,
Should you stop to think,
Why a young girl's beauty,
Should be tarted to the brink.

What need is there for make up
On young unblemished skin.
Cheap a gentle smile becomes,
A greasy, deep red grin.

Mascara dribbled down the cheeks,
Is not a pretty sight,
When you pull up from a gallop,
In the first and foremost flight.

That youthful fresh complexion,
That is flushed by country air.
Is a simple natural beauty,
So many dream to share.

No need to gild a lily,
Its beauty is no sham.
Don't chase away your youth dear,
Enjoy it while you can.

One thing to consider,
Consider if you can.
Time enough to use that stuff,
When youth got up and ran!

Thoughts of a Timid Hunter

There goes the Demon,
The Demon of the chase.
How he loves to gallop on,
Delight upon his face!
If you're heading for a fence,
I pray you all take heed,
If, he is there behind you,
Then let him take the lead.
It is quite alarming
When flying through the air,
To be overtaken,
By this massive pair.
If there's little room for two,
To jump there side by side.
It is more than likely
His horse will yours outstride.
Its back legs can be flighty,
Respect them if you're wise.
If you trail him through the trees
Then keep well down the ride.
Displacement of the branches,
They can be quite severe.
This is what you'll realise,
If they catch you on the ear!
He means no harm to anyone,
He's a super sort of chap,
He does enjoy, when stopped to draw
To have, a friendly chat.
Though everyone is envious,
His red coat keeps so clean.

Towering above us all,
He's easy to be seen.
If he blunders past you,
Deep down in the mire,
It is more than likely,
You'll be in the line of fire,
You'll scrape the mudpack from your face,
Your mouth is full of slush,
You'll have no breath to even try,
To make the slightest, fuss.
The Demon on his seventeen two,
My word he has his fun,
He'll turn and have a laugh at you.
You wish you had a gun!
He really is a character,
Laughter is his theme
He does make light of everything
There in the hunting scene.
You cannot get too cross with him,
No matter how you try.
So just take heed, and keep a watch,
When hounds are in full cry!

The Puppy Show

Their concentration rockets, to the huntsman's
sharp commands and biscuits in his pocket

Woodwork freshly painted, flower beds all in bloom.
The gravel raked and dampened down, hounds all well in tune.
White coats neatly laundered, bowlers blacked and buffed.
Kennels looking spick and span, yards all neatly brushed.
Arriving at the puppy show, the walkers and the guests.
Everyone discreetly prays, their puppies judged the best.
The bowler hatted squire, views the entries on the flags,
Noting conformation, rejecting feet that sag.

The puppies, unaware of pomp, their concentration rockets,
To the Huntsman's sharp commands, and biscuits in his pockets.
My hound has missed the biscuit! Picked up another scent,
Around the ring with nose to ground, he's heading for the tent.
Oh please! No, not the, chocolate cake! all laid out unattended.
While the ladies take a break, until the judging's ended. They are,
focused on the flag stones, viewing through their lenses.
I dread to think the panic if their tables get upended.

Out he comes, he makes his way, what is this scent he's found
What is so special that he hunts, his nose tight to the ground,
Oh dear! Oh, how embarrassing, I am, sitting by the ring
He's traced my scent from out the tent, in spite of all the gin.
He's promptly marked his quarry, a slobber and a grin,
Then proudly trots back to the flags, in hopes that he will win!
I say, the sheer audacity, that cheeky, handsome pup,
He always was a character, when he was growing up.

I've a rather soggy skirt hem! my hound, has hunting skills,
He's quite amused the audience, with his independent will.
The judge's hand holds high his jowl, a wry, forgiving smile.
"He's got the looks and stamina, he'll hunt a steady mile.
In spite of bad behaviour, in showing off his skills,
He will, surely hunt a fox, and push it to the kill.
His conformation, quite the tops, his heart has lots of room".
Beside a handsome present, he has won a silver spoon.

Those trying days of summer, when we take pups in our care.
Giving them a childhood, for the future to prepare.
Forgiven for their gardening, the shoes with half a heel!
I won't speak for the poor old cat, who, often missed a meal
The trials that we go through, for an invite through the post,
It's that friendly loving nature that draws me to them most.
They're loveable old softies, with, an independent air,
Some are very special, their skills we're proud to share.

Here's till
we meet
again !

The Young Huntsman

This cubbing morn, an August number,
Many folk still steeped in slumber.
The air was fresh the day was young,
A swiftly rising autumn sun.
The time of year when hunting men,
Slip nocturnal from their den.
Enthusiasm crystal clear,
What a magic time of year!

The morning sunlight rose and made,
A golden grotto in the glade.
Puppies there, some with their mother,
Explore and venture into covert.
The huntsman on his horse just stood,
As any patient huntsman should
Watched and listened to his work,
Fearful should those youngsters shirk.

The puppy with the skirters thoughts,
Who loitered there nearby his horse.
Soon was rated for his error,
Huic to them little feller!
The huntsman prays his summer task
Will show reward when hounds are asked.
The sport depends upon this man.
Today, he took his first exam.

The Old Huntsman

He's hung up his stirrups, he's laid down the horn.
A lifetime's habit, he'll rise before dawn.
He'll gaze to the spinney, a haze and a dew,
His thoughts will predict the scent and the view.
No kennels to tend to, or hounds to be drawn.
No horse to be plaited prior to dawn.
He'll tend to his chickens and chivvy his lass,
Look to his brood mare out at grass.

A faithful friend to him she's been,
She too has quit the hunting scene.
Back to the homestead for coffee and fry,
He'll relish his breakfast, a tear in his eye.
The start of the season at last has come.
No work for him, his work is done.
No cap or coat or stock to fit,
It's Barbour and boots and a deer horn stick.

The opening meet and they all arrive,
Blocking the gates on the castle drive.
Now he's a footy, abandoned his car,
He'll walk across country and view from afar.
Folk wished him well o'er a glass of port,
They prayed the new man would give them sport.
He made his way to the huntsman's stand,
Placed on his knee an encouraging hand.

His thoughts returned to his maiden day,
When the sight of the field, made him sit and pray.

He'd begged the Lord to give him strength,
To control his hounds and to clear the fence.
He had called it a day; there's time to recall,
Good days and bad days, and many a fall.
Thankful he is, and so he should.
His body is sound and his name is good.

The Lucky One

A cub came cantering down the ride,
His tongue lolled out his jaw one side.
In silence there, astride my horse,
I watched him travel on his course.

He passed us by; he'd cut it fine,
We did not dare to cross his line.
We watched him disappear from view,
And listened for the hounds on cue.

Now this young cub, had luck his way,
The scent seemed very poor this day.
While the pack worked hard on line,
Young Charlie gained his treasured time.

All unusual words Stepsau, Goodwell, Fishwier, Ty Drag, Gigman the Greg etc
are all names of fields and farms on route.

The Legend of the Bobtail Fox

(A true story)

Accounted for by Anthony Martyn, just prior to his retirement
after 25 years as Master/Huntsman of the Glamorgan Fox Hounds in 1986.

Here's to the fox with the Bobtail,
Who gave us some jolly good sport,
Glamorgan will always remember
Those days from Flemingston Court.
He'd surrendered his brush to the combine,
One day as he foolishly squat,
But never again did he dither,
He cherished those parts that he'd got.
He pitted his wits with Glamorgan,
The hunt that dwells deep in the vale.
For four or more seasons he took them
Through moorland, dingle and dale.
He took them from Stepsau to Goodwell,
Through Fishwier and Gigman he sailed,
Then back up to Ross's via the Bosses,
Then down through the gorse and the rails.
He'd weave in and out like a serpent,
Through gardens and rafters and walls.
His route it was mapped to perfection,
Through holes that the hounds dared to crawl.
Down through the gardens, on to Ty Drag,
He'd linger in Halfpenny Well,
Giving hounds time, to map out his line,
A glimpse for the field there as well.
It all added fun to his capers,

The holloas that geed him away,
While Rees from the Greg, was often heard said,
"I'll get you, you bugger one day."
He'd given poor Rees such a pounding,
For years he had galloped us 'round
The scars from the hooves, were more than we'd care,
To put upon anyone's ground.
The Bobtail; his timing was perfect,
He'd had a good life it is said.
His age it would take him at some time,
Than suffer he'd rather be dead.
He'd much rather die as a Hero,
Play all his tricks to the end,
Than linger the last as a weakling,
With neither a foe nor a friend.
At this time, he was old, but still active,
The huntsman about to retire.
Bobtail, made it a day to remember,
When the oldies would run out of fire.
He gave us the slip, so the Master and Whip,
Were discussing, where they would draw.
When Bobtail appeared there beside them,
They hardly believed what they saw.
He appeared there close in the hedgerow,
Not a Corgi sat out on the front,
It was Bobtail and he was just baiting,
And tempting us all to a hunt.
Now Rees from the Greg, he went on ahead,
He rode to keep him in view,
The sound of the horn rose the hounds to the thorn,
The followers right on cue!
He led us away to the ditches,
Right handed he turned for the sea.
He took us down to the Castleton moors,

Then made his way back up for tea!
He took us right back to the Calfa,
Then the rear of the Officers Mess,
Swung right, to the west of the village,
Then over the top of the breast.
Then again the route that he favoured,
The Goodwell was pounded again,
The jumps that were there for the jumping,
Were taking their toll in the game.
A circuit again to the village,
Excitement was now at its peak,
With a twist and weave in front of the hounds,
Then over the wall with a leap.
Back to the farmyard, into the sheds,
The hounds were hot on his heels,
The absence of brush to grab in a rush,
This fox was a legend for real.
Bobtail was beat it was obvious,
As he clambered his very last wall.
Into the paddock, west of the church,
Was merely a tumbling fall.
He classed himself sure as a rascal,
He avoided the sacred ground.
Outside the wall of the church yard,
He humbly surrendered to hounds.
He died as he'd wished, he'd begged this fight.
The followers all were sad, for
We'd all become fond of old Bobtail
During the time he had had.
A silence fell on the whole of the field,
In respect of the Flemingston fox,
Who'd had his day and planned his end,
He ran us off our socks!

His mask will be cherished in Flemingston Court,
His story will always be told.
Along with the tail of the Lillyput Fox,
A legend from days of old.

*In this poem I compare the fox to a young teenage boy, who often
challenges danger for the thrill and devilment.*

The Flemingston Fox

(As told by the fox.)

I lay up in the covert, of gorse with bracken thread,
Nestled in a clearing that shelters for a bed.
Nothing there to stir me, but the pestering of a fly,
And the squalling of a seagull drifting in the sky.
Scratching there in lazy mood, with little else to do,
When suddenly a tremor of excitement rippled through.
Was that the sound of hunting horn and hounds that I can hear?
Pricking up my ears in hope, I heard it, loud and clear.

Time for me to up and go and put to test my skills,
While the hunting field enjoy, the chase with all its thrills.
I'll sit tight 'till they enter; it makes it much more fun,
I love to hear the holloa! as they sight me on the run.
I'll take them by the pasture, to set a faster chase,
Then perhaps the dingle head to slacken off the pace.
Then, back out in the open, to keep alive the game,
It thrills the field to see me; I'll lose them in the lane.

I'll dodge across the plough ground and cause them all to tire,
See their nostrils belching steam, like a smouldering fire.
I have no cause to worry; I know this country well,
I'll keep the river in my sight; it's now in autumn swell.
I'll take them through the forestry; I'll trick them in the copse,
I'll prove to those pursuing me, that I'm the wily fox.
I cause commotion in the thicket passing on my way,
I scatter mice and rabbits and birds, my normal prey.

Hounds are working hard on scent; wandered back and fore,
They've overshot the line just there, I'll rest before the moor.
Now they've hit the line again, they're screaming on ahead,
I'd best to put my best foot fore, or I'll be surely dead.
I will head on down the railway line and out across the moor,
I'll stir the stinking ditches and thread the rushy floor.
I'll aim to keep my head low where rushes fail to shield,
For I intend to lead these hounds for years across these fields.

I will head now for the river, there's no crossing bridge in view.
That will cause the fainter hearts to form a British Queue!
Slipping in below the bank, I make my way down stream,
While getting out beneath the oaks, I hear their distant scream.
I will climb into the branches, concealed in shaded hue,
The branches dense protecting me, in my grandstand view.
Hounds now hot upon the line, their music loud and clear,
While in the distance I can see, hard riders drawing near.

All intent upon the chase, the fever at a pitch.
An odd top hat emerges from out that stinking ditch.
Those that clear it show much skill, others jump it blind.
There are a few I must admit, get sadly left behind.

The scene is quite exciting; it's picturesque to see,
The red coats and the black coats and hounds, pursuing me!
Some are riding chestnuts, some on smart big bays,
Some all clipped and plaited especially the Grays!

As they cross the river a youngster plunged right in,
Really, it's amusing see a topper take a swim!
The rider scrambles up the bank, you've guessed it, soaking wet.
That horse it dumped him neatly, my word he's in a sweat!
They've lost my scent, their casting wide; light is fading fast,
They blow for home, a thrilling sound, you see! I'm safe at last.
I pride myself upon my skill; I have the right to jeer,
I have survived to tell the tale, to return another year.

I'll make my way cross-country when twilight comes in low,
Feed myself upon the way, weave my way quite slow.
I haven't had a bite all day the vermin soon will roam,
I'll gently pounce upon my tea as I am strolling home.
Perhaps when I am old and frail, time will take its toll,
I will fail to catch my prey from off the forest floor.
Then hounds will be the victors, and put my soul to rest,
I will go, were foxes go, the famous and the best.

Trials of The Hunt

We hear in all the hunting songs,
The pleasures of the chase.
Little is there sung about,
The trials of the pace.
Those who ride a seasoned horse
Are sure of pleasant days,
Not so good the rider, who
rides one with tiresome ways.
Then there is the youngster,
As green as green can be,
Inclined to get his rider,
Neatly wrapped around a tree.
Who comes across a jump, that he
Has never seen before.
Not at all unusual,
Puts his rider on the floor.
All of these are bridges,
We all must cross in time,
On the patient journey, that
Takes a youngster to his prime.
When he's seasoned to his tasks,
The fun! And oh, the smiles.
The pleasures that we sing about
We dreamt of as a child.

The Mighty and the Mouse

When the horse is in the stable,
Steeped in comfort from the storm.
A mouse sits on the manger
With the hope to share his corn,
Who avoids the hall of plenty
With the fear of finding bait,
Dines in safety in the stable,
Though he sometimes has to wait.

Do you think the horse would worry?
The fact he has to share,
Or grateful for the company,
He's glad to see him there.
Perhaps it kills the boredom
Watch him scale the stable walls,
This tiny little fellow, who's
A mere whisker tall.

Whatever is the feeling, twixt,
The mighty and the mouse,
I rather that he shelters there
Than shelter in my house.
I do not think the quantity
That satisfies his needs,
Would be the slightest worry
To, the horse that shares his feed.

The Hunting Scout

High on the hill, hear his distant cry,
His cap is waving against the sky.
Tighten your girth, secure your cap,
Look to your reins and take up the slack.

Soon on the line in haste we will fly
Charlie is viewed by his piercing eye.
Who would deny him the right of the way?
The man that has viewed the quarry away.

He is the one, who speeds up our sport,
Just like a guardsman looks out from his fort.
This is a man, who will ride at great speed,
His knowledge is one that the huntsman will heed.

Unlike the waving, holloas and cries,
The huntsman has hailed him from numerous sides.
Which causes the coolest of tempers to boil,
When hounds are intent there to work at a foil.

That's my master

The Gift of Seeing

One cannot miss God's precious gifts,
When riding in the vale.
The beauty that's bestowed on us,
Such wonders never fail.
We travel on the same old road,
We've travelled it before
But those that have that special gift
They see a lot, lot more.
Once those, inner eyes awake,
New pictures will unfold,
Living in a brand new world,
That's different from the old.
Those who have the gift to see
Can capture changing scenes.
While others merely cast a glance
They have no time to dream.
They barely care to look around,
They think, they've seen it all.
But what a pity, that their eyes,
Don't really see at all!
They do not see the detail, or
Completely understand,
What makes this countryside of ours,
A pleasant, healthy land
Urban influx leaves a mark,
Discarded beds, settees,
Bags of garden litter dumped
A thoughtless beast is he.
The keepers of the country side
Must deal with all the mess,
That we can ride the countryside,
And enjoy it, at its best.

Hunting folk

When you lie awake there thinking,
Of the season that's ahead.
The hunting that will take you,
In the darkness from your bed.
Sheer excitement with a tingling
That is flowing through your veins.
One never gives a single thought
To winds and driving rains.

One never seems to worry,
All the pressures it entails.
Keeping work and pleasure,
In the balance like a scales.
Your business and the family,
And still, before the fun.
Horse and tack and stable work.
Each day it must be done.

Damn it! does it matter?
We have no time to slack.
Each single ounce one gives to life,
Is two-fold given back.
That is why, the hunting folk,
Right across the land
Will rise there very early,
To meet the tasks in hand.

The Hunt Ball

A vision stands before me, elegant and shy,
What depth of sheer beauty, flash within those eyes.
Tenderness and gentleness, swells from deep within,
Lines of classic beauty, sweeping to her chin.
Her hair, it shines like threads of gold, picking up the light,
Venus? This is Venus, Venus come to life!

Perhaps it is the whisky; I haven't had a gin,
Or the glass of champers that has put me in a spin.
For here before my very eyes, a beauty to behold,
Pass another glass across, that I might feel so bold
To approach this lovely vision, ask her for a dance.
She could be, just for me boys, a little more than trance.

Her dress, with dainty frills of lace, trimmed with seeds of pearl,
Pin tucks of the purest silk, set graceful folds awhirl.
This vision stands before me, driving me insane,
Pass the bottle over, I need courage for this game.
Encouragement to capture, Miss Venus for a dance,
This Hunt Ball lads, I think, could be my very biggest chance.

A partner of my very own, replacing tot and glass,
Exactly what I'm looking for, a touch of sheer class!
The only thing that bothers me, is my inebriated state.
Do you think she will accept me, if I ask her for a date?
If I pull myself together, she should be quite impressed,
I hope she is as beautiful, less my whisky and her dress.

The Farrier

The music of the anvil
As the hammer, strikes its blow.
Sparks from out the fire,
Like a golden fountain flow.
Horse shoes on the rafters,
Midst cobwebs, on display.
Here's a man who shows his skills
In every working day.
The true art of the fitting,
Is what cheers him as he works,
Not a task that any man
Could find the room to shirk.
A tangled heap of metal
Lying on the floor,
An upturned horseshoe fastened,
For luck upon the door.

An upturned horseshoe fastened,
For luck upon the door.

He works amongst the coal dust,
With a leather cladded lap,
With power in the forearm
And muscle in the back.
A true and honest craftsman,
Worked there from a boy.
Every shoe secured,
Is to him a perfect joy?
His work is hard and heavy,
With the element of risk.
The spells he taps into the feet,
Are lively, sharp and brisk.
His are skills we cherish,
For Farriers second class,
Make our days a misery,
And limit us to grass.

The End of the Day

The Huntsman raised his hunting horn, the blow for home was shrill.
Across the misted valley the resounding echo's trill,
The field split up, they bade good night, the huntsman made his way,
With the hard core of the field, to end a perfect day.

At a point where tracks divide, we bade them all good night,
As we rode the dingle path, we watched them out of sight.
A satisfying picture of the huntsman and the whip
With hounds all gathered into heel, to make the final trip.

They headed up the valley, across the facing bank,
Riders, mostly riding slack, in order of their rank.
As we rode the stony bank how clear the voices sound,
Stretched across the valley as we were homeward bound.

Enjoying now the gentle hack, discussing of the day,
Parted from the hunting staff, now half a mile away.
We heard the sound of hunting horn, ring clearly o'er the brow
As if controlled by dead man's break! We stopped to listen - Wow!

That sound from in the distance, does tingle in the blood,
It makes you want to gallop back, as if before a flood.
There again the music came; we heard it loud and clear,
Just calling in a wayward hound, so homeward on, my dear.

A gentle touch upon the rein, a slight squeeze to the side,
The horses get the message as we put them back in stride.
The ending of another day, the homestead now in view,
A bran mash greets the horses, but for us, a good hot stew.

The Change of Time

Gone are the days of the country squire,
Whose wealth and lands spread far.
Who lead the field in direct line,
Over hedges, ditch and bar.
In hot pursuit of the hunted fox
When hounds were in full cry.
They crossed the land in a fevered band.
The obstacles they'd fly.

Never a care to the crops had they,
As long as hounds gave tongue.
But rated and swore, if galloped
O'er, purely for the fun.
Times and fortunes now have changed,
The squire's lands dispersed.
More farmers free of landlord's chains,
But tightly chokes his purse.

They milk their cows and furrow their brows,
As owners of their land.
They pride their crops and fence their stock,
With wire, strand for strand.
So now the line rides not so straight,
It's ridden more with care.
To heed the crops and cull the fox,
The countryside to share.

The hunt has gone through many an age,
Through changing scenes and times,
Politics have intervened,
And tried to tow their line.

The country folk must carry on,
Preserving country life.
Let's hope the children yet to come,
Will hunt, without the strife.

Limericks

A Countryman living in Crew,
Longed to hunt through cobwebs and dew,
So, he stepped on a train,
Swapped a horse for his crane,
Then over the shires he flew.

It is a magnificent sight,
To study the stars in the night,
It's a countryside pleasure,
For stars light's no measure,
For town life with bright neon lights.

A Ride on the Sand Dunes

The sand dunes roll ahead in gold and green,
Cascading slopes and peaks of mystic dreams.
Monuments of storm and wind blown free,
Conceal a hidden pathway to the sea.
A Wilderness, where horse and riders play,
A sheltered haven taken for the day.
Where horses feel the magic of the wild,
And grown men here, are liken to a child.

What is the magic in these mystic hills?
Excitement wrapped in devilment and thrills.
We find the hooves will scarce to touch the sand
As tail and mane blow free here, strand for strand.
This is where our tensions disappear
Never giving time or thoughts to fear,
Where one becomes as supple as a stream,
Thus binding horse and rider to a team.
It's here we gain the freedom that we seek,
Where breezes, brush the freshness to our cheeks.
While riding on forever to the sun
With fleetness of a deer on the run.
The horses, simply bounding to the peaks,
Liken then to Pegasus, winging to the deep.
It's here on times, when sailing through the air
With cat like spring, they find a leg to spare.
When gaining contact safely with the sand,
They gallop on, the moment that they land.
What confidence we have here in our mount.
Who seems to have more legs than we can count!
And all awhile, alert they swerve and sway
From gorse and rabbit holes, peppered on the way.
While on and on we ride, o'er hill and dale,
Like waves that romp and toss before a gale.
Until we see that gem, within our reach,
The quietness of, that secluded beach.
With miles and miles of pure and fresh washed sand,
Which stretches out ahead in bold command.
It's here we race and gallop to the sea,
To plunge into the waters cool and free!
Where horses prance and shy as the foaming waves go by.
These are such happy memories for me.

Amateur Entertainment

So many folk conceal a gift,
With modesty they ride.
With hidden natural talents they
Are riding at your side.
You think of one as pleasant, or
Perhaps a big Buffoon!
Never had you realised,
He could sing in perfect tune.

There's the dainty, shy young lady,
So sensitive, demure.
Quite capable of dosing sheep,
Or lambing down a ewe.
But had you ever given a thought,
Of how this damsel shines,
When coaxed upon a curtained stage,
Reciting Shakespeare lines!

We've ballet dancers, cancan girls
Musicians of the best.
All clothed in cloaks of modesty,
Riding with the rest.
The coffers need replenishing,
A Panto'? or a show?
One only has to plant the seed,
To watch the talent flow.

We get a little hassle,
Each one has different views.
The nerves and fears of amateurs,
Throw others off their cues.
The babble in the dressing room,
The make up and the threats,
Ladies tearing 'round in bras,
Squeeze into tu tu nets!

Then the Master sang a solo,
When, suddenly, a blank!
His glasses in the dressing room,
Oh my! His heart it sank.
Specks arrived from everywhere,
With panic on the stage,
While lost amongst the laughter,
He had lost the blooming page.

A friendly bunch of amateurs,
The mishap stole the show.
And set amongst our loyal friends,
It caused the mirth to flow.
We thank that glass of courage, that
Had driven their fears to ground.
And when the great applause resounds,
The smiles replaced the frowns.

A Hard Day

Day, what a day, When we took a fox away,
Never dreaming of the pace or the distance of the chase,
Like a never-ending race,
The steady one stayed tracking all the way.

Hunt, What a hunt! With the fox, way out in front,
From the time that he was found, aimed to run each horse to ground
To the music of the hounds.
The fox, that every sportsman longs to hunt.

Safe, very safe, was my feeling in the chase,
Astride a known schoolmaster, going every moment faster,
She did everything I asked her,
She's a favourite and I knew she'd keep me safe.

Sound, very sound, as we raced across the ground,
With the fences fast approaching, it's as well she needs no coaching,
Although the ground was poaching,
I just knew she'd land with four feet on the ground.

Grand, really grand, was that feeling of command,
As we fast approached the Master, only wishing he'd go faster,
His mount gave all he asked her,
The time had come to need an extra hand.

Speed; super speed, as I caught up in the lead,
When the Master gave permission, to take over his position,
With my horse's disposition,
It was then; it seemed my horse was losing speed.

Drive; need to drive; now I really had to ride!
For it's quite a different matter, when you're out beyond the Master,
With no lead to draw her faster,
It's times like this you really have to ride.

Heed; need to heed, When you're settled in the lead,
When the pack is out of vision, and the path is your decision,
Choosing fences with precision,
Yet all the while intent to hold your speed.

Prayed, how I prayed, but my faithful one, she stayed,
Just in time to see the pack, take a right swing off the track,
As I saw them double back
And I view them to the covert, in the glade.

Pride oh what pride! There was no one at my side,
As I witness their success, as they laid their prey to rest.
It was time to turn back west
Taking news back to the Master full of pride.

Horse, what a horse! I appreciate of course,
She would soon to fade away, if I rode like that each day,
My! She had the power to stay,
I appreciate the efforts of my horse.

Sides, heaving sides, with the nostrils blowing wide,
It is time to take it steady, someone else must now be ready,
Should that huntsman need a neddy!
Should they flush another fox from down the ride.

Preparation

Summer's gone, the time has come,
To tone those sturdy limbs.
To get both horse and rider fit,
And so the bellies trim.
The walk outs and the uphill trots,
Along the country lanes,
But first of all, we pass the stage
Of aches and muscle pains.

The scenery magnificent,
The valleys calm and still.
The little streams are flourishing,
How rapidly they spill.
The oak leaves gold and copper toned,
Are brilliant in their strife.
Just like the candles final flare,
Before they quit their life.

Those fruitful days, roll swiftly by,
Preparation now complete,
A build up to the pleasures of
The sport and racing fleet,
We'll cosy up those winter days,
With horses stabled snug,
Enjoy the daily exercise
With, the comfort of a rug.

Foals

Some are none too dainty,
Others are petite

Some are very colourful,
Others rather shy,
Some are bolder than you'd like,
They'll stare you in the eye.
Some are none too dainty
Others are petite,
Some are flighty that's for sure,
But all are rather sweet.

Lesson No. 1

Do not jump your way home at the end of the day,
Do not do what I did; just do as I say!
Such was the day, when my head hung in shame,
I took a good lead o'er a jump of great fame.
A jump that out hunting, took many a toll
Under trees a deep ditch and a telegraph pole.
To jump it when jostled, with thrusters behind,
Was something that never had entered my mind.
Here was a chance, just a few hacking home,
A Master to lead us, my spirits in tone.
The mare seemed intent, determined to go,
The very last minute said "no, no, no, no!"
What is that cavern, that shadow, that ditch?
It was then I sailed over, to show the old witch.
So here is the moral to this little tale
When hunting is over don't jump any rail.
Your horse will be tired; you're well under threat.
It's you'll be the laugh, in the ditch, soaking wet.

*'Twas then I sailed over
to show the old witch*

Limericks

A young man went hunting, be blessed,
Was thoroughly bored with the dress.
So he brightened his tack,
With bright red and no black,
Then galloped along with the rest.

A vicar who took up the reins,
He prayed as he hunted the lanes
But fell at the dyke
Dear lord what a sight,
And suffered the pride and the pains.

A thruster who rode with the Curre,
Had said to the Master "O Sir",
If you let me go first,
I'd no need to curse
Or punish my horse with my spurs.

At this the Master replied,
I think you have skin like a hide
Ride rough shod o'er me
And soon you will see
Your spurs will be banned from the ride.

There once was a man who wore braces,
Who walked with such airs and grimaces,
Till one day in the ring,
Came a chill to his grin,
As his trousers restricted his paces!

There was a young lass with blond hair,
Who certainly knew how to swear.
The filly she had,
Could be equally bad,
And dumped her with grace, in the square.

The Piebald Mare

Who dares to call me Gypsy

Who said I am a gypsy,
Because my colours gay?
With stamina and sturdy bone,
I've strength to pull a dray.
I'm reliable and loveable
I turn out every day.
I'm a goer, I assure you
With a jump as good as they.
Who dares to call me gypsy,
Or mock my foot and feather.
I'm as lucky to my master,
As a sprig of Scottish heather.

Opening Meet at the Castle

The Castle looms midst wooded scene,
To hold our gaze with constant dreams.
What memories could these walls unfold,
Of times gone by, if truth were told?
The sleepy drive 'neath oak and beech,
Meanders till the fortress reached.
As our thoughts go dreaming on,
We're soon aware how time moves on.

As there above this peaceful scene,
A roar of engine breaks our dream.
The airport, built along the way
Soon jolts us back to present day!
Here we have a scene that's set,
This rat race briefly we'll forget.
As horse and riders mill around,
It brings a bustle to the grounds.

The red coats and the turn out neat,
Makes nineteenth century scene complete.
A lifestyle of the past revived,
The castle once again alive!
The Host and Hostess of the seat,
Give welcome to the Opening Meet.
How clear come memories of the past,
A pity that it cannot last.

When every one has had their sup,
And tilted up the stirrup cup.
The Huntsman blew his hounds away
The scene returned to present day.
A Jumbo took off overhead,
Nineteenth century now was dead.
Progress must not be delayed,
The points against are much outweighed.

Still, we have a way of life,
That eases modern stress and strife.
Are we not glad traditions last?
To help keep memories of the past.
And so tradition must go on,
Don't let's forget the life that's gone.
Never from this lifestyle sever,
It must go on, yes on forever

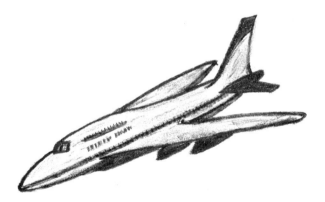

A Jumbo took off over head
Nineteenth century now was dead

Chairman of the Hunt Supporters

He's head sherang of raising funds,
Head sherang of tents,
Head sherang of Portaloos
Of transport and of rents.
How could they do without him?
Do they ever stop to think?
Do they know this loyal goffa?
Hauls the glasses and the drink
He's organised the washing up
The dinners and the talks,
He's sorted out the raffle
He has hired the knives and forks.
Of course he has his helpers,
Yes, a very loyal band.
Though strange it is, that certain jobs,
Will slip through all their hands.
So it is the chairman,
That stays behind there late.
Clearing up those tiresome tasks
And locking up the gate.
He's often seen out hunting,
In his top hat and his red,
Could be called off to a puncture,
Before the hounds go home to bed.
For sure, he is mechanic and
The transport head sherang,
Who else then could they send for,
When the tyre goes off bang.

It's the honour of being chairman,
Who takes up all the flack.
What amazes everyone,
He keeps on coming back!
To take up his position,
As loyal as before.
Chairman of the hunt supporters,
Prepared to take on more.
So all you hunting people,
Who do enjoy the sport
Appreciate the workers,
Who graft, to run the fort.

A Light Hearted View

Hunting is enjoyed by all the field in different ways,
Some intent to cull the fox, with hounds they closely stay.
Others get their thrill and fun, watching hounds at work,
Intent on all the signs and sounds and where the fox might lurk.
Some go purely for the ride, to have a friendly chat,
Others love to jump and chase, while some hack at the back.

If you keep in with the field, rightly so you should!
You're apt to lose the sight of hounds, especially in the wood.
Amidst the chatter on the field, the music can grow faint,
So patiently, we simply must, sit around and wait.
Unless your very brave and bold, to wander from the field,
To risk a well earned blistering, which brings you back to heel!

Patiently, we bide our time and join in with the chat.
Until we hear a holloa, or see a waving hat.
We all admit, we get good fun amongst this friendly crowd,
Although at times it aggravates, if voices get too loud.
You keep a sense of humour, partaking of the fun,
But always keeping sharp an eye, in case the fox should run.

The sort of thing that happens, would raise the huntsman's brow,
Surely he would sympathise, when scent is rather slow.
We get ambushed in the covert, when the hounds
have drawn and gone,
We get Dallas as a bonus, while waiting to ride on.
You get cocktails if you sample all the flasks that float around.
Especially if the day is cold and quarries gone to ground.

You get chaos at the fences, except the few elite,
Those that have the natural gift or have the perfect seat.
Peppermints and chocky bars, like fishes and the loaves,
Are shared amongst the multitude, devoured by the wolves!
There are even toasted sandwiches that ooze with raspberry jam,
Get shared amongst the chosen few, resist them if you can.

Amidst the great excitement of riding in the chase,
The straining of the eardrums, should hounds flush out a brace.
We get varied types of pleasure and humour through the day,
We battle with the elements, and try to mind our ways.
Everyone has different views; perhaps it's just as well,
If all our minds had single thoughts,
There'd be more fun in hell!

TAKE HIM! He's a bully!

A Stormy Morning

They lash the rain against the panes,
The autumn winds at dawn.
Not an unfamiliar sound,
A late September morn.

Our thoughts betray our eagerness,
To rise up from our bed.
The tack is clean the horse is green,
The quilt we're forced to shed.

Once we've reached the stable yard,
No thought of turning back,
Excitement overrides it all.
We're glad we did not slack.

Then as we travel on our way,
Through grey and dismal scenes,
The eeriness of early dawn,
Through wet, transparent screens.

Branches swaying in the wind,
The leaves all in a spin,
Multitudes of stormy clouds,
The autumn's well set in.

There, arriving at the meet,
The faithful hardened few,
Horses not turned out as yet,
Their woolly coats in view.

The faded caps, the shabby boots,
The best still stored away,
Everyone is all intent,
Upon the task today.

Training hounds to enter,
Cubs are moved around,
Dispersing all the litters from,
Their summer breeding ground.

The rain may fall; the wind may blow,
Young horses on their toes,
Regardless of the weather,
The Huntsman always goes.

The eeriness of early dawn

Uncontrollable Excitement

A mist hangs in the valley,
The air is rather chill.
The lorry with the hounds arrive
Their tongues speak loud and shrill.

The hunter in the stable yard,
He prances, side to side.
His ears are pricked, he trembles, as
He blows his nostrils wide.

There's little doubt within his mind,
The task that we're about,
He paws impatient at the ground,
Longing to get out.

What is the magic in the voice?
Of hounds before a meet,
That boils the blood of many a horse
And electrifies the seat.

A part of us, that nature bred,
So deep within our souls.
The natural instincts, man and beast
Find hard to self control.

There's the
Pick of the
Litter, but
the little one
goes to the
kindly home!

The Right to Hunt

It is with sheer excitement,
That we rise with the early dawn,
Anticipating horse and hounds
And the shrill of the hunting horn.
Little do the town-folk know,
Will they ever understand?
What joy, a cold damp morn can bring,
To the keepers of the land.

We plough, we till, we thresh, we mill,
Tend the flocks on the barren hill,
Control the brambles, gorse and fern,
On footpaths that, the towns-men yearn.
The countryside is here to share,
With those who seek the country air.
A landscape that is kept in hand,
By he who prides his plot of land.

And all he asks in fair reward,
Is to hunt his land in true accord,
A leisure sport, that's known to prove,
A healthy wildlife, through and through.
They're not extinct, not diseased,
They roam the land, just as they please.
But, God forbid, should it be banned,
What a cost to our sacred land!

A State of depression
The thought of
being parted!

Part Two

Country Verse

A walk in the Country

Reflections

If you walk along the tow path,
Or wander by the lake.
Water green and murky
Massed with ripples from the drake.
Reflections all distorted,
Shimmer in the sun,
Duplicated cottages or
Children having fun.
A subject for a photograph,
A classic for my book.
Shade and light reflecting
A double rick and stook.
Then all at once, they vanish,
As clouds will form a screen.
Reflections, like a mirage,
They vanish from the scene.

Cardiff's City Saints

St. David's with its Medic's,
St. David's, Festive Hall.
St. David's shopping centre,
Where the tradesmen rise and fall.
Where the bustle of the shoppers,
And the drag of tired feet
Are broken by the shrieks of youths,
That rush in off the street.
Weaving through the shoppers
They echo through the halls,
Where Gareth Edwards motionless
Clutches at the ball.
A lively scene from off his plinth,
Though few may glance his way.
In that city rat race fever
That erupts at break of day.

A City, rich with elegance,
A capital renowned.
A joy to every tourist
With its castle and its grounds.
Museums full of treasures.
It's fountains and its halls.
Fit for any nobleman,
That pays a stately call.
The market place, the hostelries,
The bars, the clubs, the banks.
The docks piled high with timber.
The coal, the ships and tanks.
A host and hive to industry
The hubbub of the vale,
The very heart that pulsates,
Those arteries of Wales.

I am just a country lass,
Who pays infrequent calls.
Who cringes at the bustle,
Admires the castle walls.
Rows and rows of fashions,
A maze from which to choose.
Drawn towards the elegance,
Of frills and dainty shoes.
Then, weary from the tension,
Like a fish that's out of sea.
I sicken at the prices
Of a single cup of tea.
Returning to the countryside,
I ponder at the gate,
And marvel at the stamina
Of the hardened city saints.

Drawn towards the elegance of frills and dainty shoes

The Countryman's Tales

A dog on ahead and a dog at his side

The countryman lives, by the twitch in his tail!
There's many a sign there's many a scale.
Tales that are handed from father to son,
No one quite knows when they ever begun.
Rhymes that we never would care to forget,
Whether the summer be dry or be wet,
Or if the heatwave will end in a storm,
Whether the rain will arrive before dawn.
Then there are threats of the winter being hard,
Berries abundant, it's well on the cards.
Ice in November that carries the duck,
Assures us the winter' be all mild and muck.
The countrymen knows every sign every sound,
Birds high in the sky or low to the ground.

A red sky at night, not in the morning,
Shepherd's delight, not a shepherd's warning.
There is, no one nearer to God than he,
And no one is blessed with a heart so free.
The sun is his watch, the stars are his guide
A dog on ahead, a dog at his side.
There is no one, who asks so little from life,
Home and a hearth with a good loyal wife.
The tales that they share are second to none,
All handed down from father to son.

We Do Remember

Marching past the cenotaph
That cold November morn'.
How deeply some remember
The days those boys were born.
Heroes, who gave all they had,
That we might still enjoy
This good old land called England,
They loved so as a boy.
Loved so much they gave their life,
While others gave their sight.
Many still bear painful wounds,
Of battles, day and night.
That's why we still remember
We keep one special day.
In our hearts we love them all,
But sad they could not stay.

Satisfaction

When the roses of the summer
Shed their perfume on the breeze,
Sprays of brilliant colour,
Cast a spell upon the bees.
We with satisfaction sit
And reap our true reward.
Tools are neatly stacked away,
We've polished up our sword.
The battles have been harsh and tough,
We've fought the vicious thorn.
Kept disease and bugs at bay,
Up at early dawn.
Forgotten are the hardships,
Not a single care occurs,
As we take the perfumed air,
And listen to the birds.
Walking in the garden,
Our trug upon our arm.
Snipping at the faded blooms.
Rejoicing at the charm,
Of a garden full of roses,
Cascading from the bowers.
Giving our retirement,
Some very happy hours.

Think of the seas with the billowing sails

Pleasures and Pastimes

Pleasures and pastimes have we all,
Some to the sea have heard the call.
Some go golfing thrice a week,
Or climbing mountains, to the uttermost peak.
There's soccer, rugby, take your pick,
Some love the thrust of the hockey stick.
Think of the seas with the billowing sails
Cheeks all flushed with the wind and the hail.
Whatever our pastimes choose to be
Up in the air, on land or sea,
They call for effort, strength and strain,
So often they will cause us pain!
Still we come home well refreshed,
The cobwebs blown from off the chest.
Pleasures and pastimes keep us sane,
We care not a toss, for the wind and the rain.

Contentment

I strolled along the footpath,
I gazed at waving corn.
I listened to the seagulls,
That sailed like ships in storm.

I stood upon the cliff top,
And gazed way out to sea.
Who is there here to envy?
No-one, only me.

Born into the country side,
I cherish what is mine.
Freedom and the wildlife,
Sunshine and the brine.

A pair of hands to master,
The tasks that lay ahead.
Time created just for me,
With time to rest my head.

Contentment in my pleasures,
Grateful for my skills.
What more is there to wish for but
Good health with all the frills.

I stood upon the cliff top and gazed way out to sea.

Tranquillity

Oh to live a tranquil life,
Where tempers don't exist.
Frustration rolls off everyone,
Just like a rolling mist.
A world where words like tiredness
Are hard to understand.
Happiness and pleasant smiles
Are always there to hand.

Living on a razor edge,
Is not a pleasant way.
Weighing up each little word
Before we have our say.
For fear it should ignite a spark
Inside a frustrate soul.
Perhaps it's rest is far the best
Find this elusive goal.

A Sign of Rain

Swift is the swallow that dives down in play.
Skimming the yard on a hot summer's day.
Wild is the sheep dog, who springs for a catch,
Sorry to say he's a very poor match!
The swallow, dives low and catches the fly,
Doggy is left with a sad looking eye.
Still he keeps trying, again and again,
A very sure sign, we are in for some rain.

The pleasures of living in a sleepy country village.
No bustling traffic before dawn,
When one can rise and take in Nature's true beauty.

A Pathway to Heaven

The snow fell silent in the night.
The dawn beheld a brilliant light,
When to the window to behold,
A land of white, a sky of gold.
In haste I dressed and downward sped,
Welcomed the dawn in its blanketed bed,
Donned my boots and made my way,
Down an untouched path at the break of day.

How blessed was I, to be the first
To dent the snow and capture the thirst
Of the rising sun, in a tinted sky,
Only the birds, the sun and I,
The dainty trail of a homeward fox,
Veering off, through a hedge of box.
The sky, now streaked with pink and gold,
The air was fresh and crisp and cold.

The village slept, the curtains closed,
A muted crunch beneath my toes
Here in the road I gasped with glee,
With pictures painted on every tree.
Trees and shrubs in the gardens flushed,
Like icing from a frosting brush.
This roadway here beneath my feet,
Pathway to heaven in a, silent street.

Oh why must everyone arise?
And break this spell beneath the skies.

Tarnishing pictures I behold,
As sheep lie safely in their fold.
Yet, how could I so selfish be?
To keep these moments, just for me.
Then, as I see the curtains drawn,
I bid goodbye, to my perfect morn.

The milk and postmen all arrive,
Blemish the paths up every drive.
The dogs come out to romp and roll,
While bleary eyes come out to stroll.
Cars are cleared of their mid-night thatch,
Every door has a lifted latch.
The children snowball on the lawn,
This is the picture after dawn.

I turn myself upon my track,
And start my homeward journey back.
As my footsteps are retraced, I'm
Hailed and jeered, by the snowman's face.
The children laugh and romp in fun
While birds they search for every crumb.
The paths are cleared with spade and brush.
My pathway to heaven has turned to slush.

The footprints of the homeward fox.

The Country Child's Weather Glass

The tiny little pimpernel,
Its dainty scarlet flower,
Brightly shines and smiles at you,
Through all those sunny hours.
Suddenly, it turns quite shy
When rain clouds start to form.
Droops its head and shuts its eye
To shelter from the storm.
If he sleeps, then take your coat,
Although the sun may shine
For that's the little fellow that
Will warn you well in time.
Delicate and dainty,
It is classified a weed,
I am always pleased to see it,
Scattering its seed.
We see it in the stubble fields,
And in the veggie patch.
It's the country child's own weather glass
And always up to scratch.

The Master Artist

The sky displays the pictures,
Of an artist bold but shy.
His canvas full of changing scenes,
As clouds go drifting by.
A Master who portrays his mood,
So boldly with his brush.
Stormy days, his style is harsh,
His paintings bold and flush.

Wintertime, his scenes are grey,
The shapes are wild and stern.
As the sun comes shining through,
You see, his mood will turn.
He'll brighten up those morbid scenes,
With frills of brilliant light,
His works become exotic
While Action scenes delight.

Those special paintings on an eve,
When snow lies on the ground.
As the sun goes down to rest,
Deep reds he'll splash around,
Phantom glows, they're colourful,
The paintings rich and loud.
Above an earth that slumbers,
Beneath its winter shroud.

On clear, bright days those watery scenes,
A sign of rain to come.
He sketches fans of water beams,
Rising to the sun.
How tastefully the colours glow,
Just as a storm has passed.
That brilliant coloured rainbow,
Its beauty ne'r surpassed.

This artist has a preference,
As to shades throughout the year,
Blues and whites are favoured,
In summer days so clear.
A little dash of grey brushed in.
To take away the glare.
With little tints of silver
Reflected here and there.

His chariot bright, like burning fire,
Sinking in the west.
Giving us a gentle wink.
It's nearing time to rest.
The crows are homing in to roost
Against his backdrop pink,
The stock draw to the water hole,
To take their evening drink.

How he loves to use those shades,
Of brilliant pink at dawn,
Looked on by the shepherds,
As fearsome threats of storm,

I'd love to be an artist,
As original as he
With skills in blending colour,
And sweep of arm so free.

On summers days, a clear blue sky,
Without a single stroke,
I sometimes think about him, has
He stopped to have a smoke?
Those little tell tale puffs appear
Like dainty cotton balls,
I'm sure that he is resting in
His, vast celestial halls.

Whatever time of year we find,
This artist will perform,
Creating such a masterpiece,
Through daytime, dusk and dawn.
And we can all be sure, that
Whenever we're awake,
We see his exhibition plain,
There will be no mistake.

I Envy the Sun in the Morning

I envy the sun in the morning,
As it rises over the plain.
Splashing the sky, with silver and pink,
When dawn has rejected the rain.

The mist that hangs in the valley,
The cattle that low o'er the lee,
I envy the sun on his journey
As he spans the land and the sea.

The sheep as they graze on the hillside,
The rivers meandering by,
Oh, what a view of the landscape
As he journeys across the sky.

I envy the sun in the daytime,
As I watch the clouds roam free
He looks on the world with never a care
He has never a thought for me.

I envy the sun at twilight,
As he sinks in a bath of gold.
The fiery red, as he goes to bed,
When the night-time will unfold.

Who'd envy, the moon at night-time
As he takes his light from the sun;
He lights up my room at bedtime,
But I will arise with the sun.

A Quiet Corner

There's a quiet little corner,
On land that's all my own.
Where someone in the distant past,
An acorn once had sown.
I have been the lucky one,
To Witness, its success.
To the one that sowed the seed,
I can but humbly bless.

For in this quiet corner,
Where I sit and sip my wine,
There stands a grand old oak tree,
That has known a span of time.
And in that space has stretched and stretched,
Its branches far and wide,
It reaches for eternity,
Approached on every side.

To look up through its branches,
A cathedral, nothing less
With wooden pews for choir boys,
Ah, natures very best.
The breeze a welcomed organist,
Accompanies those birds.
Though, you must be there all alone
To, understand the words.

It's rendered by an artist
And flushed by setting suns
That splash it with a magic glow,
And dabble it with fun.
While spirits of the countryside.
They all come here to dwell.
Beneath its giant canopy,
They brew their mystic spell.

Patience

Patience is a treasure,
A treasure to behold.
If it has been granted you,
Then guard it just like gold.
Many long to have it,
Try just what they may,
Though they persevere,
It runs out, every day.

Fellows of the Soil

(Childhood Memories)

In the hay field turning, shaking,
All the corners needing raking,
Children romping, laughing, aching,
While the swallows swoop and dive.

In the root field hoeing, thinning,
Backs were bending not so willing,
Rows ahead seemed endless stringing,
While the larks they sang on high.

In the cornfield cutting, reaping,
Stooking sheaves to dry for keeping.
Children scratched with stubble shrieking,
While the wildlife slipped away.

Those were jobs I well remember,
June, July until September,
Fellow of the soil a member,
As the seasons made their way.

Farmer
Ted reckons,
"They're all
home bred"!

Praise to God

I rise up in the springtime,
To the chorus of the dawn.
To tend a ewe that's nurturing
A lamb that's newly born.
We've rain to fill the ditches,
We have sun to warm the land.
It does not always please us,
We would like it on demand.
Summertime we cast our eyes,
On lawns the trees and bowers.
Breathe the smell of new mown hay
And honeysuckle flowers.
There are poppies in the cornfield,
And flowers on the sedge
Larks are singing in the sky, while
Fledglings flutter in the hedge.
The cobwebs wave and shimmer
On the pastures after dawn.
A mist hangs in the valley,
On a peaceful, autumn morn.
We cannot yet imagine,
All the spiders that would yield
The silver chiffon mantle,
That could span a massive field.
Wintertime the air is cold,
Our cheeks are flushed and red.
Glad now of the harvest store,
There's livestock to be fed.
The trees are stark and naked,
There's a frost within the sod,
Every season has its reason
For this, give praise to God.

The Anguish of Drought

There's time enough, since they have known,
The feel of falling rain.
Fresh, green pastures now no more,
Have turned to barren plains.
Deep cracks have long since gaped at them,
From out the sun parched clay
The desperate farmers tend their stock
They dread another day.

As streams run dry, the rushes fade,
The drought brings early fall
The murky shallow rivers,
Polluted, merely crawl.
Helpless now they realise,
The cause of all the pain.
Nothing more than absence,
Of God's refreshing rain.

What happened to the equinox?
That filled the flowing dykes.
What happened to the thunderstorms?
That appear oft' at night.
What happened to the showers?
That April always spared
What's happened to the Lord above,
Who listens to our prayers?

Summer Drought

The sun shines down on thirsty lawns,
Sun baked pastures, wilting corn.
Flowers swiftly fade from bloom,
The babbling brook has lost its tune.
Water holes are cracked and dry,
Everyone resents the fly.
How we all just long for rain,
Sunshine loved becomes a pain
Never do we like excess,
Especially when our green's suppressed.

2001

Lottery mania- I declare!
Who wants to be a millionaire?
Scratch cards fall from every pack,
The Christmas sock is now a sack.
Mobile phones, they rule the day,
Have they thought who has to pay?
Spending well beyond their means
Causing nightmares, frantic dreams!
Swipe cards getting out of hand
Isn't this a crazy land?

A Nature Reserve

The railway lines of bygone times,
Where trains have ceased to run the lines.
Apple stumps thrown by the way,
To fruitful trees have grown today.

Here birds and wildlife find a piece,
Where foxes breed in safe relief.
Midst butterflies and rambling briars,
Where rabbits never seem to tire.

It's here a host of wildlife live,
It has so much that it can give,
A little haven made by man,
Completed by deserted plan.

STUBBORN

A Weird Imagination

Imagine that the world was stripped,
Of every single tree.
Cabbages all walked about
On legs like you and me
Flowers non-existent,
Fish all ruled the land
And not a man amongst us
Possessed a single hand!
Ears were deaf to pitch and tone,
Musicians never born
And every loving animal
Had coats all made of thorn.
Colours all were shades of grey
The seas all full of dust,
Food was but a single pill,
No tooth to eat a crust.
Can you just imagine?
What our life would be.
A horror thought,
I could not bear
Not even just to see!

Beautiful Things

The world is full, of beautiful things,
Roses, cobwebs and butterfly wings.
Flowers that bloom, with the sun on their lips
Dewdrops that shine on the sweet petal tips.
Birds with bright feathers that glint in the sun.
Starlings and peacocks, to mention just some.
Goldfish and dragon flies, down at the pool,
Puppy asleep in the shade keeping cool.
Smiles on the lips, that give pleasures untold.
Pictures on windowpanes, frosty and cold.
Cherubs, with rosy red cheeks in the pram,
Smiling to show his first tooth when he can.
All of these pleasantries, everyday things,
Music, voices and choirs, that sing.
Why, do we ever have moments of gloom?
Soaked in self-pity face like a prune
Surely in hours of darkness you'll find,
Beautiful thoughts to cheer up the mind.

Earthly Paradise

At the open window,
In the evening of the day.
When temperatures had risen
To a peak of summer's play.
A day when all the animals,
Took refuge in the shade
We all simply sat and sipped
And looked a little jade.
Sitting at the window,
With the shutters open wide
Was like an earthly paradise,
Your partner by your side
Taking in the evening air,
In peaceful mode, content.
The moon peeped through the branches,
As he made his steep ascent.

Clear, the noises drifted
On the waves of evening air.
Peaceful sounds, that rid us,
Of troubles and of cares.
The bleating of the sheep and lambs,
The flight of owl and bat.
A whirl of moth wings in the air,
The purring of the cat.
Sitting at the window,
With a satisfying sigh,
Gazing at the heavens
In a starlit studded sky.

The face and body glowing
From the rays of mid-day sun.
This was like a holiday
With workday rolled in one.

Friendship

Friends are there to cherish
Many come and go
Seeds of friendship perish
Others sturdy grow.
Those are friends to count on
Stand the test of time,
Share in all your troubles,
Always being kind.
Keeping all your secrets,
Joining in your fun,
Changes not as time goes by,
Whatever they have done,
Understand your feelings
Pleasure in your skills,
Never show resentment,
Though some are bitter pills.
Rejoicing in your triumphs,
Helping in your need,
That is then a true friend,
A lifelong friend indeed.

My Garden

In looking back to days of youth,
If I should, really speak the truth.
My garden seemed a mighty task
And of my time too much would ask.
At busy times it would grow wild,
Just like an unattended child,
Then share a little time once more,
How soon its neatness would restore.

When my household chores depressed,
My garden then I humbly blessed,
How my heart with pride would burst,
When I had quenched my fresh air thirst.
It's not symmetrical you know,
Nor did perfection ever show.
A private garden, rather shy,
Though, very pleasing to the eye.

Where grew the old and new alike,
And many weeds allowed to strike,
As long as they remained in place
And had a somewhat pleasing face,
Then, perhaps they would survive
And raise their heads unto the skies.
Gardeners, would likely shudder,
I would swop it for no other.

Our Modern World

This is a crazy mixed up world,
With problems, far and wide.
The continents that suffer drought,
Their stock and children die.
While here in Britain rain more rain,
Where floods can bring despair.
What is wrong with our world?
What's happening up there?
Are we all so thoughtless
That the good Lord, shows his rage
Or, we think we are so clever
We do not plan each stage.
The balance, sliding off its spool,
By science and its use,
Regardless of the consequence,
We treat it with abuse.
Perhaps we all should stop and think,
This rat race brought by greed.
To be content with what we have,
And live more by our creed.
We've never had a life so good
The mods and cons are nice!
But there again, so true to life,
We have to pay the price.

Peace

Company, is wonderful,
Companionship is great.
Though on times one can feel,
That company can grate.
Play upon you harshly
When you need a little time,
To have some peace and quiet,
To sort, things on your mind.
When you have obtained it
Your mind is clear and fresh.
Then you are prepared to face
Good company, and jest.

Optimism

There's a peace and there's a haven,
To be found within your soul.
If you can shelve your worries
To let your skills unfold.
Be it painting, be it writing,
Tapestry or sport.
Offering a helping hand,
To, less than able folk.
Then, time is lost it lingers not
It brings you much reward,
Worries seem a trifle,
If you, strike that active chord.

Trying not to linger,
Or wallow in a trough
Your problems then are liken to
A very trivial cough!

Perseverance

We all must persevere
And try to reach our goal.
Standing up to challenges
However tough or cold
We all must aim to practice
To achieve and to amend,
Practising and practising
To the very end.
Persistent perseverance,
Will attain the highest grade,
Failing that we will I'm sure,
A better man, have made.
One who's practised tactics,
Academic or in sport
Stimulates the brain to learn
Although we may fall short.
What more is there to aim for,
Than the best that we can give
Never are we proud of
Being liken to a sieve.
What a great achievement,
Knowing nothing's gone to waste.
In talent or in effort,
In confidence, or grace.

Precious Moments

Heavenly is the early morn,
When birds in chorus hail the dawn.
The cared for lawns all mown anew,
Faintly silvered by the dew.
The sun is rising in the east,
The early bird enjoys his feast.
Flowers raise their heads with grace,
To greet the sunshine's new born face.
Shadows, streaked across the lawn,
That's the picture after dawn.

It's then I like to take my break,
Before the family all awake.
To wander on the lawns alone,
Seeing how the plants have grown.
While rooks in chorus all compete,
In icy dew I bathe my feet.
That is when I'm free of care,
Before the telly starts to blare.
Cool and fresh, it's perfect bliss.
Moments I would hate to miss.

ALL GONE !

The Wonderful You

Oh for the voice of a nightingale,
The face of an angel fair.
Accompanied by a pair of hands,
That would calm yet the wildest mare.

Hands to embroider the finest thread,
Stitch the most delicate seam,
Coupled with this, the most delicate gift,
Of spinning an intricate dream .

Oh for the brain of an intellect,
That flows with absolute ease
Spill from the mind, poetical lines
That no other man could exceed.

Then to be given a lions heart,
One of the gentlest strain,
Yet to be blessed with graciousness,
And achieve a respected name.

Then parcel all with a gift of charm,
To make up a wonderful you,
Would life be really a paradise?
Or a muddle, what gift to pursue?

The Wonders of Spring

Clumps of golden daffodils,
Beneath the wintry tree
Wrestle with the cold March winds,
A vicious brute is he.
We watch them in their struggle,
Despondent at their plight
Wonder if they'll have the strength,
To last, another night.
As the new day dawns afresh,
The storms and gales have passed
Twigs and broken branches
Littered on the grass.
The flowers look bedraggled,
A little worse for wear,
But quietly unnoticed,
How nature does repair
As the daytime passes,
The sunshine fills the sky.
Birds all in a fever
Repair their nests on high.
The air again is filled with spring,
Everywhere serene the
Daffodils once more they stand
As, graceful as a Queen.
Perhaps you'll see on looking close,
A blemish on the petal.
Like us all as time goes by,
A line or grey hair settles.
How those daffodils they shine,
And brighten up our day,
Clumped beneath that naked tree,
Where lambs just love to play.

As the flowers pass their prime,
The tree with life anew,
Gives birth to brilliant foliage,
Concealing all from view.
With grace the branches sweep down low
Beneath their new born weight.
Unnoticed now, those daffodils,
Decline to mortal state.

The Working Bee

How the bee he toils undaunted,
Every little flower head haunted.
Sips the nectar sweet and clear.
Manufactures for the year,
Honey that we all desire,
Enjoyed on toast beside the fire.
I marvel at his mammoth task,
Collecting all within his grasp.
Of the pollen he will spread,
While in the dainty flowers tread.
It's hard to realise his worth,
He's such an asset to this earth.
Oh please I pray protect the bee,
From careless use of sprays we see.
Not a risk that he deserves,
For keeping us throughout the years
With honey for our pantry store,
A treasure shared from shore to shore.

Weary to Bed

Steeped in a cloud of mystical dreams,
Engulfed in polyester.
Snug to extreme in the down of the duck,
An adventurous siesta.
As sheep skip by, I drift away,
To a land of great intrigue,
Where plots are never ending,
And races lack in speed.
When terror looms, the feet hold fast,
Weighted more than lead.
The pillows turn to solid walls,
About my frantic head.
The sheets become a hunter's net,
That bind about my limbs
Yet never am I captured,
In these nightmares, for my sins.

A Secure Bird

The tree stood firm, with outstretched arms.
The bird flew to its breast,
Secure there, it settled in,
Its cosy moss-lined nest.
Puffing up its feathers as it
Snuggled deep and low,

The evening breezes rocked the bough
Gently, to and fro.
While there, in sweet contentment as
The darkness came in deep.
The breezes hummed sweet lullabies,
The bird dropped off to sleep.

Imagination

What instils a poet
To conjure up, such dreams?
What sets the mind in rhythm?
To spin out reams and reams
Of words with special feeling,
That ripple off the tongue.
Simple words in grand array
To, thrill the hearts of some.
Words, that like an artist's brush,
Paint pictures in your mind.
Pictures of such detail
All woven through the lines.
Those that have this special gift,
Although they may be shy.
I think, have something richer,
Than a millionaire can buy!

Why

What travels through the toddler's mind?
What pictures do they see?
When all intent to understand
As, well as you and me.
The questions that they ask us,
We answer best we can
But little does it satisfy,
This quizzing little man!
There always seems a loophole,
In the answers we supply.
Which causes all these toddlers,
To produce, another why?
They never seem content to hear
The answer plain and brief
We underestimate our babes,
Well, that is my belief!
Their urge to learn and understand,
Far greater than their size,
And that is why they do produce,
Innumerable whys!

DUCKS HAVN'T GOT TEETH !

Night Noises

Walking through the country lanes
Homeward in the night.
The noises of the countryside,
They echo out of sight.
Many a time I've walked alone
From Girl Guides or the like,
Up the lane across the fields to
View the farm in sight.

The moon when shadowed by the clouds,
It cast an eerie light,
Then suddenly a clearing,
And everywhere is bright
In and out the shadows,
As I walk beneath the trees,
The ripples then a rustle as
The wind sweeps through the leaves.

Steadily I made my way,
Venturing the night
The hooting owl, I'm sure would give,
Many a child a fright but
All this to a country girl,
Is just a common fair,
Never a though that swooping bats,
Would tangle in my hair.

The noises of the night time,
One really can't predict.
Depending on the weather, or,
Who takes a moonlight flit!

One thing known, at depth of night,
When sight is rather dim.
Our hearing sharpens to a pitch
Responds to every whim.

The one noise, that I must confess,
Did make my blood run cold.
It's when I heard the vixen call,
It pierces the soul!
Though it is familiar and
I know what to expect,
She never fails to churn my blood, or
Cause a pounding chest.

The colours of the night are bland,
Just hues of black and grey.
In winter time the stormy clouds
Are racing by the way
And when I'm at my journey's end.
These thoughts lie deep in me,
If I were not a country girl,
How petrified, I'd be.

Depending on the weather or
Who takes a moonlight flit.

Foot and Mouth Epidemic 2001

The horror of disease can wipe out a lifetime's achievements and pedigree breeding stock,
that have taken years to build up to a quality and standard, to satisfy the demands.
Then for those who have worked tirelessly to keep their animals free of the disease, that
they should incur a loss of, a year's income and financial hardship through restrictions.
When compensation is an easy option for those who make no effort.
Life can be brutal!

There's a deep depression drifting in the valley.
The slaughter men and vets, they make their way.
The stench of disinfectant, fouls the nostrils,
While ministry officials rule the day.
It's an army of destruction that's attacking,
An innocent and unprepared foe,
The noises of the shotgun, the thud of falling stock,
The silence in the dairy, the absence of the flock,
The thrilling sound of new-born lambs silenced by the scourge.
The cowman broken hearted, pining for his herd.
Farmers' hearts are breaking; their sibling's eyes are sore.
A lifetime's efforts taken, with a threat to many more.
The bank officials tighten, the noose about their neck,
As the livestock farms are cleared, the fields an empty deck!
They cannot turn to arable, the quotas won't allow,
Clear of stock they all must be, a year or so from now.
Country folk and nature, walk there hand in hand,
Bringing life into the world, and tending all the land.
Carers of the countryside, suppliers of our bread,
There's a silence in the countryside; the livestock lots are dead.
Disease we know can venture to the hearts of undeserved.

Officialdom has fanned the flames, and forced an upward surge.
Bureaucracy has taken hold, has stifled able men,
Who know the task and understand, but do not push the pen.
While the carcasses are stacked there, waiting for the word,
Disease transported through the air, carried by the birds.
While little men with clipboards and a superficial air,
Cause desperation, suffering to farmers in despair.
There are biers, there are fires, there's a stench of burning flesh.
Smoke to span the countryside, a gutting nasty mess.
The stench of rotting carcasses, laying on the yard,
Waiting for the ministry, for orders, that is hard.
Some farmers like the phoenix, yes; they will rise again,
Their dedication to their work, they will survive the pain.
There is no other life for them, no other way they know,
For others, it is far too late, to build another show.

The Innocence of Youth

Youth, is like a bursting bud,
Protected by its sepals.
Thinking they're a flower in bloom,
On which the bee might settle.
While looking in the mirror,
They see beauty there supreme.
But only time will prove to them,
How innocent they've been.

> More sound, the words of wisdom come,
> When time has waved its wand.
> Wild the words of youth will seem,
> Like bubbles on a pond.
> As each little bubble bursts,
> And youth still babbles blind.
> Another petal opens up
> And still the mirror's kind.

By the time the bloom is full,
They've gained a lot of ground,
They find their words compared with youth,
A little more, profound.
As the age increases more,
Their wisdom now replenished.
Then they're rather sad to see,
They've now acquired a blemish!

> They, now see youngsters as the buds,
> As they themselves have been.
> A wilting bloom appreciates
> Each age hands out a dream.
> Not one of us can go through life,
> Perfection all the way.
> Once we've gained experience,
> Then youth has had its day!

The Problems of a Poet

Have you ever lain there listening,
To the stillness of the night?
While all around you slumber,
When the bat has taken flight.
The shadows of the storm clouds,
They float across the moon,
And cast an eerie darkness on
The stillness of your room.

You lie there and you ponder
Rhyme and reason rolling by.
Wonder why, you cannot sleep,
However hard you try.
As long as rhyme is rolling,
Rolling through your head.
Never will you slumber
In the comfort of your bed.

So you rise into the darkness
And let the lyric roll.
Take a pen and paper,
And write it on a scroll.
Once the verse has tumbled,
Free and fluent from your head,
You will slumber soundly,
In the comfort of your bed.

A Child's Concern

When you're at the seaside,
Does deceit live in the eye?
I see, on the horizon,
Where the water meets the sky,
The sun is sinking in the west,
It lowers by the hour.
Then, as it meets the water line,
It sinks without a shower!

No one tries to save it,
As it sinks into the brine.
All that I am thankful for,
It isn't one of mine!
They must be, rather plentiful.
For there I see next day.
Another sun, will brightly shine,
Then drown, the same old way.

Summer after summer,
From the beach, I've seen them sink.
Obviously they cannot swim
To vanish in the brink.
The thing that bothers me the most,
Is, no one seems to worry.
I am sure that they could save it,
Those Life Guards, if they'd hurry!

Our Country Church

The squeak of iron hinges,
Then groans the big oak door.
As it opens in, we see
Rich carpets on the floor.
Gothic arch and windows
With tiny leaded panes.
Colours, rich in different hues
With bible quotes and names.

All in dedication there
Of ones who've gone before
Open up before us as
You enter through the door.
Rows and rows of polished pews
With hassocks on the floor,
Where Christians knelt in murmured prayer,
For centuries, or more.

Books of hymns and common prayer
All musty stained with age.
A bible born on eagle's wings
Lay open at the page.
A brilliant window facing east
Above the altar high,
This is where one's overcome,
A presence, drawing nigh.

The cross upon the altar,
Reflects a beam of sun.
The flower ladies handy work
Arranged by someone's mum.

Come here on a Sunday, when all glad voices sing.

Just a tiny country church
With rafters high and bold
Where Christian spiders spin and weave
The air is still and cold.

There are cassocks in the vestry,
Jam jars on the bench
Polishes behind the door
To aid, the cleaning wench.
The organ keys are silent,
The sunbeams filter in.
Come here on a Sunday
When all glad voices sing.

Spring

Season of youth and brilliant greens,
Newly unfold from winter's dreams,
How we have longed through darker days,
For warming suns and grass to graze.
Now as winter fades away,
Our hopes are raised with every day.
Pruned are the weak, we're fresh to start
As life goes on, with stronger heart.

What determination there, the new born foal
The proud, proud mare

Filled with hope our spirits strong,
Depression now replaced by song.
We rise to fight and gain reward,
Like soldiers with a shining sword.
All the birds will chant and sing,
The daffodils, they herald spring.
The little lambs, a sight to see
While on the banks, they frolic free.

What determination there,
The new-born foal, the proud, proud mare.
His long legs spread in all directions,
Nudged by mother's strong affections.
We chuckle just to see him struggle
His legs get twisted in a muddle!
When he gains that firmer stance,
It's little time before he'll prance!

These are wonders of the spring
That rid us of the winter's sting.
Enthusiasm rising bold,
We now forget the winter's cold.
As each day brings growth anew,
And Maytime brings the early dew,
The trees with blossoms, full array
It lifts the spirits for our day.

Sell by Date

Most things grow, mature,
Then decay without much fuss!
There is a sell by date on most things,
A sell by date on us!
There are buildings, there are cheeses
And children from all walks,
Earls and Kings and labourers,
Who work and think and talk.
We all grow to maturity,
God willing reach our prime,
Eventually we pass our best
Then start the slow decline.
Fulfilment is maturity.
Those pleasant, twilight years,
When we except, we've had the best,
And done with sweat and tears.
We have age, we have experience.
Gained knowledge through the time.
Though energy and stamina,
Now, that is in decline!
We try hard not to think of it,
We fail to see ourselves.
What chance have we of beating youth?
When put out on the shelves,
There are generations rising
Blessed with skill and blessed with brain,
Let them receive their just reward,
Let's loosen up the reins.

Those of us who've passed our prime
Should savour and enjoy,
Give a hand and share a heart,
Encourage girls and boys.
So we will keep our dignity
While, holding good our name.
To go down, in the register,
Good subjects, some of fame.

We all grow to maturity

A Break

A Vintage car perhaps to drive
A bicycle or horse to ride

Your home life may be happy,
Your work you quite enjoy.
But all of this can sour if
You haven't got a toy!
A vintage car, perhaps to drive.
A bicycle or horse to ride,
A dog to take you off on walks,
The W.I. with monthly talks,
Or, simply just a game of golf,
Ballroom dancing, samba, waltz?
Watching birds and wildlife play,
Moulding pots with messy clay!
Whatever is your choice of game,
It really helps to keep you sane.
So set your work upon the shelf,
For a while, become yourself.
Your problems will not seem so great,
When you have had, a little break.

An Outburst

The goods shown in the window,
Are, not always, true display.
Of a person in an outburst,
There is far more tucked away.
The things that hurt one very deep
Are drawn behind the blinds.
The little tantrums that escape
Just hint, a state of mind
Of, something there, much deeper,
So deep one cannot know.
For they are far too personal
For a gentleman to show.
And if you then can realise,
The one that bears the blow,
Are, the nearest and the dearest,
With the hope it doesn't show.

Avoid the one in the big hat!

Christopher William

Christopher William a sturdy young chap.
Who bounces and wriggles on Grandmother's lap.
He's sturdy of stance with strength of an ox
His legs we'd be proud of in red rugby socks!

A short little neck, a head hard as steel,
When taking a bump he seldom will squeal.
A right little lion yet tender as lamb,
I'm sure he will grow to a handsome young man.

Now Christopher William his eyes are so blue,
Although at this time he barely makes two.
He's topped with a thatch of ash blond hair,
He whistles away and he hasn't a care.

That smile with a twinkle your heart will be sent,
The kisses he gives your forced to relent.
Everyone knows how Grandmother's praise,
I'm sure he will grow to have gentleman ways.

The Countryman's Stick

Whether it be cherry or whether it be nut

Grown as a sapling, straight as a dye,
Offshoot of its elder, reaching for the sky.
Whether it be cherry or whether it be nut,
Cut off at a level, or taken at the butt.
When taken by a craftsman,
With skills, he will refine.
Put in splints and seasoned
Until the proper time.
You can bet a dollar, results will be superb
With a silver collar, and the handle of a bird.
Maybe just a thumb stick, to help you on your way
One with fancy carvings, to keep for market day.
Could be, it's a shepherds crook,
That's mounted with a horn.
The one that I would favour most, is
The thumb stick cut from thorn.

Stormy Waters

We all decry our country,
If e'r the going's tough.
Not always count our blessings,
Take the smooth path with the rough.
Whatever meagre living
Repays our days of toil,
It is a special honour
Being carers of the soil.
So let's keep up traditions,
While producing for the needs.
Facing all the storms that hit
The countryside and seas.
Fisheries and farming
Are dedicated toils,
To feed a nation cheaply
While managing the soil.
Room for all aboard the ship
Who work to earn their keep,
Frustration is the demon
That stirs us in our sleep.

A Lost Love

"It is better to have loved and lost
Than never loved at all"
I quote the very famous words.
We readily recall.
To lose a friend or partner,
A pain one has to bear.
A pain which turns to loneliness,
With no one there to share.
Evenings never ending,
The social life grows thin,
Time alone will heal the ache,
The smile's a temperate grin.

As time goes by, the road will turn,
Surroundings seem anew,
Meeting different people,
They have different points of view.
When you've turned that corner,
And joined another crowd,
Who knew you not as one of two,
It helps to lift the shroud.
Here one finds new happiness,
A change, and different scene.
A life that's not to be compared
With what your life has been.
You make the most of what you have,
With old friends you recall, for
It is better to have loved and lost,
Than never loved at all.

Bits and Pieces

Home is like a shop display,
When all is toned to match,
Until we place the pieces,
To which we are attached.
Arranging all our treasures,
However big or small,
Together with our photographs
And pictures on the wall.

Bits and pieces, they're the things,
To make a home complete
Quite different from the other homes
You find along the street.
Some to glass and silver draw,
Antiques are not exempt,
Others more outrageous,
Their tastes are more contempt.

Then you have the decor,
The paint or papered walls,
The colour scheme's a massive range,
It greets you in the halls.
All in all, we're quite unique,
We each have different taste.
You feel one's personality,
When walking through their gate.

Wake up to Wales

Do come and see this lovely land

Where is this land of which I speak,
That lays so much before our feet.
A land with legends to be told
And fortresses from days of old.
Land of sunshine, land of rain
No sun parched barren, dusty plains.

It's here you'll find, neat dainty hills,
A coastline edged with scalloped frills,
Where waves, resemble trims of lace
That flounce the sands, beneath the grace
Of seagulls, in a sunlit sky.
That echoes the sound, of their raucous cry.

It's here you find rich cockle beds,
With canopies of golds and reds
As western skies are splashed in fun
With mystic light, from the setting sun.
Adorning all in brilliant hue,
As flowers sip the evening dew.

A land where Adam's purest ale,
Flows freely down through lush green vales.
Such treasure, valued more than gold,
Bubbles from caverns icy cold.
Refreshing those who stoop to sup,
Worthy of any chalice cup.

Here the hearths burn warm and bright,
To cheer us on those winter nights.
Fed with fuel, peat and coal
Dug from the heart of her rugged soul.
Wales is a nation, warm, sincere,
Friendship and kindness always near.

A land where singing fills the air,
The rafters ring in song and prayer.
Where male voice choirs thrive and reign
Their talent spread to world-wide fame.
Oh! Why does longing stir and burn
In hearts of those who can't return?

Do come and see this lovely land,
Run free upon her golden sand,
View her castles, walk her hills,
Cool your brow in the mountain rills.
Hear those voices sing her praise.
This land I speak of, it is Wales.

Home

Home is where we long to go
When we have travelled long.
Home is where our comfort lies,
When things are going wrong.
Home is our security,
When feeling rather lost.
Home is where the hearth will glow
In times of snow and frost.
Home is there to greet us
The place to which we run,
But a home without a keeper,
Is not a lot of fun.

There is not a lot of cheer
In a cold and empty grate,
Not a lot of thrill to see,
A pile of dirty plates.
Not a lot of fun to hear,
A hollow, empty sound
Telling you distinctly,
There's no one else around.
A house is just a dwelling,
Lived in just by one,
A shelter and a resting place
But not a lot of fun.

Home complete with partner,
Has a very special glow.
Lived in by a family,
Not purely there for show.

The hearth is always burning,
The kettle on the boil.
A home with love and welcome
To help forget the toil.
A house, that as you enter,
Has atmosphere and fun.
A house that's neat and lived in,
And one that's smoothly run.

One where all the family,
Respect the household code.
Everyone there takes a part
To ease, the heavy load.
Encouraging its keeper,
The home is not a drudge.
Where one has time to well refine
Those comforts that they love.
The sort of home where give and take,
Repays with love and care.
That is then a happy home,
We all just love to share.

Snails

Underneath the flower pots,
All cosy, cool and moist.
I found a grand collection
All gathered there from choice.
Tucked up neatly in their shells,
Their frothy curtain drawn.
I love to watch their tails emerge
And then their little horns.

Crawling through the flower beds,
A mass somewhat perturbed.
Moving off to find a place,
To hide there undisturbed.
They did not like the sunshine,
Hot upon their backs.
They much prefer the rain drops,
As they leave their slimy track.

Slow motion is their journey,
How intent they are to hide.
Their houses going with them,
For that slow and steady ride.
Once inside the rockery
They're safe while out of view.
They dare to venture out again,
Before the evening dew.

The Bluebell Wood

Thinking of my childhood home,
The woodland that we used to roam.
Winding paths amongst the trees,
All well trodden, sparse of leaves.
Deciduous trees, of different hues,
Standing there in crooked queues.
The sturdy trees of mighty stance,
That always drew that upward glance.
Clustered saplings there beneath,
In full attendance of their chief.
Stretching upwards in their bliss,
Searching for that sunbeam's kiss.
The plants that grew you won't believe,
As through the years the seasons weaved.
Anemones were first in bloom,
Primrose, cowslip, garlic fumes!
Bluebell carpets, splashed with sun,
That's to mention only some.
The orchids off the rides we found,
Hidden deep on secret ground.
Nestled deep amongst the trees,
Rare for, human eyes to see.
We knew their hide out! But we dared,
To tell the secret, that we shared.
The bluebells in abundance grew,
We picked them, armfuls, sapphire blue,
We took them homeward through the trees,
The perfume wafted on the breeze.
Reaching home our arms were numb,
With treasured bouquets for our Mum.
The bunches then arranged with care,
A spectacle, we loved to share.

We felt it our special right,
To roam the woods from, morn' till night.
I see it now, those drifts of blue,
The more we picked, the more they grew.

The Robin

A Robin on the path looked up
And with a plaintive tweet,
How about a crust of bread
Down here at your feet.
Those bullies on the bird stand,
They fight for every crumb,
I'm the Robin from the veggie patch
With a very empty tum'!
The ground is frozen very hard,
The worms have gone down deep.
I could bully for my breakfast,
But it would look rather cheap,
I think I'd rather stay aloof,
And keep my little patch,
Then I will keep my dignity
And manners up to scratch,
For I know you think me special!
That's why I puff my chest,
And sing to you each morning,
In my bright red winter vest.

Waiting

A Centenarian living in the year 2000, at the start of
the new Millennium. Her quality of life has
diminished, she is ready and waiting to be taken to her final home.

Caverns of emptiness, mountains of loneliness,
Thoughts flowing with anxiety.
In a mind, wrecked with age, worn with exhaustion,
Confused by an abundance of memories,
All racing to the fore, trying to relieve
The eternity of time, that each day brings.
This Centenarian, sits, waiting, longing,
For her final journey to her everlasting rest.
She has sampled the span of a complete century
And cares not to enter into the new Millennium.
This active fun loving damsel of the past,
Has cherished, an abundance of friends,
A host of companions, all gone on before her.
She was the one, who raced for the goal on the hockey pitch.
Midst cracks and jostling of hungry sticks,
All snarling and snapping at the ball.
Battling their way, backwards and forwards
In determination to regain possession.
These memories still loom forward.
There was Shakespeare, the part she played in Othello.
Still recited in her lucid dreams,
Full of the stage, this aged character re enacted,
Her school plays. Curtain! Curtain!
The curtains failed to close; she falls into deep despair,

Reality settles around her, just a cold room,
All alone, no curtains, no stage manager, no actors.
Memories of the past looming and fading.
Driving her mind into sheer confusion.
She recalls the sound of the sirens from the war years.
The whistle of the bombs, then feels the warm glow
Of the fires ignited by the incendiary bombs.
They light up her face, warm her body, then chill her heart
As she recalls the fear those fires brought in their day.
What is this confused mind doing to her?
Trying hard to comfort her, succeeding only in
Torturing her soul, confusing her brain more and more.
These things are gone and past, all but this lonely figure.
Tired and withered with age, still here waiting.
How time stands still, for one ready for that last long journey
That will take her to the land of everlasting rest.
A journey so justly deserved.

The Local Agricultural Show

Ponies by the lorry load, with kids piled in the back,
Mothers looking flustered as they race around with tack.
Jodphurs stretched to limits while others bulge and sag,
Father checks the entries as he stubs another fag.
Stewards all important as they hail the class along,
Judges frowning, worried as they view the mottled throng
Well fed ladies, bustle like bees around a hive,
Rearranging goodies, they have baked, to win a prize.

While the somewhat smart and elegant with hats and graceful pose,
Step back to make assessment of that very special rose.
They comment on the dahlias and the fragrance in the show
And did you ever dream that veg' would grow and grow and grow.
The atmosphere gets stifling, the tents are fully packed,
Folk jostling there to see the stock while others stop to chat.
Some admire the babies; some discuss the rib or ham,
While others prod and poke the wool to find the fattest lamb.

Alsations, Danes and powder puffs! All towed along on leads
Brushed and powdered, manicured, a credit to their breed.
Their owners simply plastered in surplus canine hair,
No time to groom the handlers! we must stand doggy square.
There are cattle groomed and haltered, sheep all neatly trimmed,
Really it's incredible the time these men put in.
They halter break; they wash and oil, bulls that need respect,
Arranging for the movement with a licence from the vet.

It is far from being spontaneous; it takes a lot of thought,
The secret of the feeding, the removal of a wart!
All the preparations, collecting sheaves of corn,
It draws the folk from far and wide, they work from peep of dawn.
Prayers ascend for sunshine, the car parks swiftly fill,
The organisers sigh relief, the booze flows though the till,
The winners get their prizes but the praise I'm keeping for,
The ones who made the class worth while but drew the shortest straw.

Puppy

How important is the walking,
To the puppies in the pack?
Do you think they will remember
That occasional little smack?
While growing in the freedom
With a family and farm.
We hope that they are learning,
What will bring them harm.
Playing with the old Tom cat,
They're destined for a scratch,
Discovering that hedgehogs
Can be a prickly catch.
While egging on a ewe to play,
He's butted in a brawl.
Being rough with children is not allowed at all.
With their independent nature,
They learn the world is tough,
They need to heed a rating
Or life can make it rough.
Out at walk, they're growing up,
With tender loving care,
As an individual,
A human pal to share.
Once they're back into the pack,
That's natural for their breed,
They're disciplined and happy,
With the company they need.
With individual rearing,
Human training from way back,
They will take the huntsman as
The leader of the pack.

A Late Spring

*Memories of a very hard spring. Always in farming,
you would think back of the old sayings and pray they were true.
It gave a certain strength to keep you going.*

It had been a long hard winter; the ewes had all lambed down, increasing the number of mouths considerably. Which is what farming is all about. Hopefully the better weather would soon be here. A mild spell was needed, to boost the grass and flush the ewe's milk then all would be well.

March 26th was approaching the old saying goes "Where ever the wind is on the 26th March it will remain for six weeks." Let's hope it is a westerly. As the west wind is our prevailing wind, inclined to be warm and wet. The easterly wind is cold and dry, travelling over the land.

The day arrived and to our dismay, there was a bitter east wind, ripping through the valley. The grass became dry and sparse. As the days went on, the sheep became restless, the lambs lost their bloom, they were beginning to look very dry. The gates were opened to let the sheep roam further afield, in a bid to keep them contented. Hay was fed out daily; three thousand sheep took a lot of attention in these conditions. Lambs, one of two were picked up here and there and taken into the fold for feeding as there was insufficient milk for the ewes to feed two lambs.

There was a constant bleating in the valley. The sheep were restless.

Situated in the bottom of the valley, we later experienced some late frosts, which had checked the growth of grass. This had not been evident on the surrounding farms on the higher ground.

The oak trees that had started to show a burst of bud were burnt brown on the lower part of the trees, the tops still showing the hint of young green growth. A line of the frost level could be seen clearly through the valley.

This had followed the dreaded east wind, we had had during the past six weeks.

We had, a specially good hay harvest the previous summer. The barns were full to the rafters. The old saying is "It is a bad farmer who sells his surplus hay!" Yes, we were glad of it. The other old saying is, you use half the hay by February. We had plenty we thought, but with this late spring, we had little left to spare. The old shepherd looked at the barn and smiled to himself,

"The Lord Provideth for".

The Tail End

Index

Part 1 - Hunting Verse

Part 2 - Country Verse

Further copies are available from:

Reva Publications
Llyswen, Flemingston, Nr. Barry
Vale of Glamorgan
CF62 4QJ